WE THE PEOPLE

AURA LEWIS & EVAN SARGENT

WIDE EYED EDITIONS

TABLE OF CONTENTS

★

HELLO

A NOTE FROM THE CREATORS

The original Constitution of the United States was handwritten in ink on parchment over 200 years ago and today it sits in a protective glass box in a museum. Being a very old legal document, it's not an easy read. It's full of fancy language, old-fashioned terms, and some of the loooooongest sentences you will ever see. You won't find the full text of the Constitution in this book, simply because there isn't enough room in these pages to include it all! However, we encourage (dare) you to look it up online and read it. Better yet—go and visit it in Washington, D.C. if you can.

The Constitution outlines the basic fundamental laws and principles of our government. People in law and politics still reference (and debate) its contents every day. They're supposed to, because it was written with the intention that it should be reinterpreted and revised over time as our society evolves.

The Constitution was supposedly written for ALL people who live in the U.S. However, because it was written by a small number of white men with power, we have to read it critically. We believe that if the Constitution is truly for all of us, it should be freed from its glass box and made accessible to everyone!

This book is an exploration of the Constitution. We hope it will help you understand what it's all about, and give you an overview of the practical details and an understanding of the greater philosophy that the U.S. government was built on. We have divided it into the different sections that appear in the original document. You will find some of the actual text from each article and amendment of the Constitution, plus stories and facts about each one.

Today is a major time of change in our country. We want more people to take action around the things they believe in. You can do this through community involvement, politics, activism, and so much more. We believe in the power of anger and optimism. Resistance and action. Critique, celebration, and raised expectations. Most of all, we believe that having a deeper understanding of our Constitution can inspire change. Anyone can understand how the government works, and every single person has the power to get involved and make a difference.

**WITH LOVE FOR OUR COUNTRY
AND A COMMITMENT TO CHANGE,**

Evan & Ava

Part 1: The CONSTITUTION of the UNITED STATES

The first section of this book is about the original **seven articles** (which are like short chapters) of the Constitution. It also looks at the **Preamble**, which is the opening statement of the original Constitution.

House of Representatives

RULES, NOT RULE

When the original seven articles of the Constitution were written in 1787, there were just 13 states. Government leaders wanted to make a system of rules so the states could all operate better as a team. They remembered what it was like under British rule, and they didn't want an all-powerful king or queen ever again. They were determined to create something really different—a new way to govern without one person or group getting too much power. They had already begun, and it was time to make it official.

The first seven articles of the Constitution include a detailed plan for the **democracy** that we still have today. This plan maps out who makes the **laws**, who approves the laws, what happens when there's a disagreement, who's in charge of what, how they get their positions, and so much more.

The Capitol Building

Senate

Sounds fair!

CONSTITUTION FAST FACTS

★ It was written in secret at the Constitutional Convention in **1787**, with guards at the door. In **1788** it was **ratified** (formally agreed to) by the necessary **9** states.

★ It was written in the same Pennsylvania State House where the Declaration of Independence was signed in **1776**.

★ In total, **39** people, from **12** states, signed the Constitution (see page 32).

★ The Constitution is a **legal document**. It takes the ideals of the Declaration of Independence (such as freedom and equality) and transforms them into legal principles.

In the following pages, you'll read about **Congress** and its two parts: the **Senate** and the **House of Representatives**. Here, the **Capitol Building** in Washington, D.C. houses the offices of Congress, with the Senate on one side and the House of Representatives on the other.

THE THREE BRANCHES of GOVERNMENT

★

The Constitution outlines the structure of the U.S. government right at the beginning, in the first three articles. Before we dive into the details, here's an overview of that structure.

The White House is where the president lives and works.

THE THREE BRANCHES

The government has three branches: **legislative** (Congress), **executive** (the president), and **judicial** (the courts). Each has power over the other two, so that no one branch can overpower the others. This system can seem inefficient sometimes, but it guarantees a balance so that no one small group of people will have all the power.

BALANCES? CHECK!

The three branches need to discuss, debate, and sometimes argue with each other in order to make decisions about laws, war, policy, and everything else. Debate is good! It means that different sides of important issues are considered, and that no one person decides for everyone. This is called a "checks and balances" system, and is a key to a democracy that works.

PRESIDENT
(THE EXECUTIVE BRANCH)

This branch is made up of:

- the president
- the vice president
- the cabinet.

The president has the power to sign (approve) or veto (reject) **bills**. The president also acts as commander-in-chief of the U.S. military and police, who have the power to enforce the law (make sure everyone obeys it!).

COURTS
(THE JUDICIAL BRANCH)

This branch is made up of:

- the Supreme Court
- other **federal** courts.

The courts have the power to settle disputes and make sure laws are being upheld—and that they're following the framework of the Constitution.

The Supreme Court Building

The Capitol Building

CONGRESS
(THE LEGISLATIVE BRANCH)

This branch is made up of:

- the Senate
- the House of Representatives.

Congress has the power to write bills (proposed ideas for laws) that sometimes become laws.

To find out more about how a law is made, turn to pages 18 & 22.

WHAT DO YOU THINK ?

If you could be in one of the three branches of government, which would you choose and why?

Washington D.C.

The Power of an Individual

★

THE LILLY LEDBETTER ACT OF 2009

This is an example of when the **three branches of government** come together to change the law. Near the end of her career at Goodyear Tires, Lilly Ledbetter found out that she was being paid less than her male colleagues for doing the same job or even more. No fair! In 1998 she sued Goodyear for **discriminating** against her because she was a woman.

The jury decided in Ledbetter's favor, but there was a sticky point in the existing law that brought her case in front of the Supreme Court. The law said she could sue for discrimination **within 180 days**, but it was unclear when that period should begin. Ledbetter argued that it should **reset with every paycheck** that she earned less than the men she worked with. Goodyear thought it should be 180 days from the time the decision to discriminate was made, when the first unfair check was given to her (back when she just started her job in 1979!). In 2007, The Supreme Court sided with Goodyear and Lilly Ledbetter lost.

Then things got really interesting, and here's where the three branches come in:

> " *It is fitting that with the very first bill I sign—the Lilly Ledbetter Fair Pay Act—we are upholding one of this nation's first principles: that we are all created equal and each deserve a chance to pursue our own version of happiness.* "
>
> **PRESIDENT BARACK OBAMA**

1. SUPREME COURT

The court interpreted the law in favor of Goodyear. Ledbetter lost. But then, Supreme Court Justice **Ruth Bader Ginsburg** (see more about her on pages 25 and 75) made a dissenting argument (a strong disagreement presented after a court decision is made). She claimed that Congress never meant the law to be interpreted this way, and asked them to change it. This was a rare and powerful moment of one branch calling out another, to do better.

2. LEGISLATIVE

Lilly Ledbetter worked hard, using her now-famous name to **petition** Congress and fight for the law to change—even though she could never benefit from it, now that she had lost her case. For the next two years, she spoke out as an **activist** about the issue of **unequal pay**. She didn't want this to happen to anyone else, and she used her voice as a citizen to make change.

3. EXECUTIVE

President Barack Obama believed in Ledbetter's case, and they supported each other while he was campaigning for president. He spoke of her case and equal pay, and she spoke in support of him for president. When he was elected, the **Lilly Ledbetter Act of 2009** was the very first bill he signed into law, clarifying that the 180-day period now resets with every paycheck. This is a big step towards equal pay in the workforce.

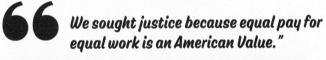

> *We sought justice because equal pay for equal work is an American Value."*

LILLY LEDBETTER

THE GENDER & RACE PAY GAP

The Lilly Ledbetter Act of 2009 was a huge step forward in the fight for equal pay. But it's not over yet! For many reasons, there is still a significant gap in salaries for women across the board, and even more so for Women of Color. At the top of the ladder are Asian women, who earn about **97%** of what white men make. White women earn 79%, Black women make **67%** and Hispanic women earn **58%**. (Note: Men of Color also make less than white men. But there are gaps within communities too: Black women make **89%** of what Black men earn, and Hispanic women earn about **86%** of what Hispanic men make.)

To read more about the connection between gender and race, see "Intersectionality" on page 88.

A GUIDING LIGHT

★

The Constitution doesn't list all the laws for the country, but it does provide a framework for making them. It's designed to prevent the government from making a law that goes against our rights and freedoms. Think of the Constitution like a lighthouse, guiding our government towards shores of justice!

JUST IN CASE

When someone feels their constitutional rights have been violated, they can tell the government about it. Their statement or argument is called a case. When a case makes it all the way to the Supreme Court, it can be instrumental in changing the law. Cases become great stories that help us understand how it all works, and how our lofty laws actually affect everyday people. Judges can look back at decisions in old cases to help them decide on new cases. Cases made by regular people set new standards and can really shake things up.

POWER: THE GOOD, THE BAD, AND THE UGLY

The Constitution is all about power. Power means, simply, the ability to do something or act in a particular way. In a democracy like this one, every single person has power to influence the country. The Constitution was written with ideals of equality for all. But, in our country, a person's power has historically depended on who they are and what they look like.

From the very beginning, the U.S. was built on putting some people first, and hurting others. Native Americans were here first, before the American government drove

them from their land. They didn't even gain citizenship until 1924 and couldn't vote officially until 1948 (though they weren't really able to in many places until 1965 with the Civil Rights Act).

Racism was at the heart of the United States' founding in many ways. Power has not been distributed equally and today we still face inequities in our society and our government.

We can work to bring more and more equity to the political system!

PARTY TIME!

Parties are groups of people within a political system who share core beliefs and goals. The American political system is considered a two-party system, dominated by the Democratic and Republican Parties, which have been around for more than 200 years (though they have gone through many changes). There are other parties too that are smaller, like the Libertarian Party and the Green Party.

Sometimes the party system can lead to problems with checks and balances. For example, if the president and the majority of the House are members of the same party, they are less likely to "check" each other when they have shared interests. Then, it's up to the courts to do the checking. The Constitution does not mention the parties at all!
Why do you think that is?

WHAT DO YOU THINK

Anyone can start a political party! If you could start a party, what would it be all about?

FUN FACT!
DONKEY *V.* ELEPHANT

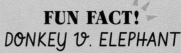

The Democratic Party is represented by a donkey, and the Republican Party is represented by an elephant!

THE PREAMBLE

Signed September 17, 1787. Ratified June 21, 1788.

★

"WE THE PEOPLE OF THE UNITED STATES, IN ORDER TO FORM A MORE PERFECT UNION, ESTABLISH JUSTICE, INSURE DOMESTIC TRANQUILITY, PROVIDE FOR THE COMMON DEFENSE, PROMOTE THE GENERAL WELFARE, AND SECURE THE BLESSINGS OF LIBERTY TO OURSELVES AND OUR POSTERITY, DO ORDAIN AND ESTABLISH THIS CONSTITUTION FOR THE UNITED STATES OF AMERICA."

The **Preamble** comes at the very beginning of the U.S. Constitution. This one (very long!) sentence lets us know why the Constitution exists, what it intends to accomplish, and who it's for. **Let's break it down:**

WE THE PEOPLE

At the time these words were written, "We the People" was not really inclusive of everyone. Today, can we interpret these words to include ALL people in the U.S.? What do you think?

UNION

The states have a lot of independence, and yet they also operate together as a "Union." That's why it's called the "United States."

JUSTICE

This means that fairness and equity—for all people—is at the heart of the Constitution.

DOMESTIC TRANQUILITY

Domestic means "at home." The Constitution helps keep the peace among the states. No fighting!

COMMON DEFENSE

Protection of the United States' people and property is the responsibility of the federal government, not individual states.

GENERAL WELFARE

This is the well-being of the people in terms of basic needs, such as food and shelter.

BLESSINGS OF LIBERTY

Liberty means freedom. With freedom comes certain "blessings" or benefits, for example: the freedom to express yourself, worship as you choose (or not), and have free access to information. *What would you consider some other "blessings of liberty"?*

OURSELVES & OUR POSTERITY

The Constitution is designed for us, our children, our children's children, and on to our great, great, great, great, grandchildren . . . and beyond!

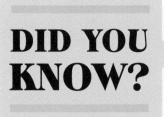

DID YOU KNOW?

There are whole dictionaries dedicated to words that only appear in legal documents like the Constitution, and which you hardly ever hear in regular speech. "**Preamble**" is one of those words and it's just another way of saying "introduction." In this book, you'll find words in **bold black** text that may not be familiar explained in the Glossary on page 108.

ARTICLE 1: CONGRESS

Signed September 17, 1787. Ratified June 21, 1788. Many sections were updated in later Amendments.

★

"ALL LEGISLATIVE POWERS HEREIN GRANTED SHALL BE VESTED IN A CONGRESS OF THE UNITED STATES..."

The very first article of the Constitution is mostly about the legislative branch of the government, known as Congress.

Each state, from sea to shining sea, elects people to move to Washington, D.C. and fight for laws in Congress on their behalf. Congress is made up of two different groups called "Houses": the Senate and the House of Representatives. Learn more about both on the next few pages.

CONGRESS OF THE UNITED STATES

Congress is made up of people who talk about, think about, dream about, and endlessly discuss everything to do with making laws (turn the page to learn how!). Congress is also in charge of many other things, including taxes, the post office, the navy, and punishing pirates—just to name a few!

HOUSE RULES!
Did you notice that Congress is mentioned before the president in the Constitution? This shows that We the People govern ourselves with teamwork, and that the president is not all-powerful.

WHAT DO YOU THINK? **?**

Why do you think it's important for people in government to truly represent the population of the country in terms of race, gender, age, and life experience?

FUN FACT!
UNLIKELY LAWS

Making laws is a serious business—but sometimes they can sound pretty silly! For example, in 1948, a law passed in Connecticut that says that pickles must bounce when dropped, as a sign that they are good to eat. In Georgia, it is illegal to eat fried chicken with a fork. In Alabama, it is illegal to drive blindfolded (like, DUH?!). And in Arizona, it's illegal for a donkey to sleep in a bathtub. Better go get your donkey!

THIS IS WHAT CONGRESS LOOKS LIKE

Historically, most government officials looked a lot like the original guys who signed the Constitution: mostly men and mostly white. There has been a gradual change over the years, but between 2017 and 2019 there was a bigger shift. During that time, more women and People of Color were elected to Congress than ever before.

WOMEN IN CONGRESS OVER THE YEARS

JEANETTE RANKIN

Congresswoman
Montana, 1916

First woman
in Congress

CAROL MOSELEY BRAUN

Senator
Illinois, 1992

First Black woman
in the Senate

MAZIE HIRONO

Senator
Hawaii, 2012

First Asian American
in the Senate

SHARICE DAVIDS

Congresswoman
Kansas, 2018

First openly
LGBTQIA+
Native American
in Congress

ALEXANDRIA OCASIO-CORTEZ

Congresswoman
New York, 2018

Youngest woman
ever in Congress
(29 years)

Article 1: Congress

★

SENATE

The Senate is sometimes called the "upper" house of Congress. With only 100 members, it's pretty small. The senators get to know each other very well, especially because they can keep their spots as long as they can keep getting elected. Each state has two senators, so no state gets short-changed for being tiny—for example, Rhode Island. Read more about the Senate in the 17th Amendment on page 82.

DID YOU KNOW?

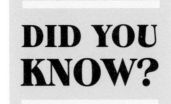

Let's say your little sister wants to make a law that schools should have free lunches. First, she needs to present the idea to her local Congressperson. If they think it's an awesome idea, they will have it written as a proper legal bill, before introducing it to the House. See "How a Law is Made" below.

◆ CATHERINE CORTEZ MASTO ◆

NEVADA SENATOR

In 2016, Catherine Cortez Masto made history: she became the first Latina woman elected to the Senate! She was raised in Las Vegas, and grew up to become the Attorney General of Nevada. She is known for fighting for the rights of women, children and seniors. For example, she is supporting bills for better healthcare for mothers and infants. She also loves nature, and is promoting a bill to protect the environment through clean energy and the use of electric cars.

HOW A LAW IS MADE

Part 1

1 Anyone can have an idea for a bill. Really, anyone! It could be the president or your little sister.

2. The bill is introduced in the House or Senate. Only a member of Congress can do this. Let's say a bill is introduced in the Senate.

3. A committee within the Senate looks at the bill together and debates it (talks about what's good and bad about it).

HOUSE OF REPRESENTATIVES

The House of Representatives is known as the "lower" house or "the House" for short. It's a larger machine than the Senate—more people, more procedures, and more committees. The number of representatives each state gets in the House depends on the number of people who live in the state. That's fair, and makes sure states with a lot of people get enough voices in government to be heard.

HOUSE FAST FACTS

★ **435** members on two-year terms

★ 20 committees, which oversee bills and laws on different topics

★ Has a **Speaker of the House**, elected by the other members, who is third in line for presidency after the vice president

★ Has the power to **impeach** an elected official (learn more on page 22)

★ In charge of **bills** about the government getting and spending money

★ **19** former representatives from the House have gone on to become president, including John F. Kennedy (see page 100)

FUN FACT!
MOM AND SON IN CONGRESS

In 1953, and again in 1963, Frances Bolton and her son Oliver Bolton both served as House Representatives from Ohio at the same time! To this day, they were the only mother-son pair in Congress.

ILHAN OMAR

MINNESOTA CONGRESSWOMAN

In 2018, Ilhan Omar became one of the first Muslim women and the first Somali-American to be elected to the House of Representatives! Omar and her family fled Somalia's **civil war** when she was only eight. They arrived in the U.S. four years later, after living in a refugee camp. From a young age, Omar had an interest in politics, and she became an activist and **advocate** for racial equality, access to education, and working families. As a congresswoman, she is particularly interested in fighting xenophobia (prejudice against people from other countries).

4. Usually, the Senate makes a lot of changes to the bill. It's rare for every single person to agree, so they vote.

5. If a majority votes "yes," the bill is passed on to the House, where it is debated and **amended** again until they agree. If an agreement is never reached, the bill dies.

6. If there is a majority in the House, the bill goes back to the Senate for one more round of debating and amending until both houses agree on the exact words.

7. Now the bill leaves Congress. Will it become a law?

See what happens next in Article 2 (page 22)!

ARTICLE 2: PRESIDENT

Signed September 17, 1787. Ratified June 21, 1788. Parts of Article 2 were updated by the 12th and the 25th Amendments.

★

"THE EXECUTIVE POWER SHALL BE VESTED IN A PRESIDENT OF THE UNITED STATES OF AMERICA."

Article 2 is all about the executive branch, which is made up of the president, vice president (VP), and their cabinet. The cabinet is a team of advisors that help the president and vice president get the job done. Think of it like a cabinet in your kitchen, filled with spices and sauces, all adding something to the meal.

EXECUTIVE

"Executive" means having the power to put plans into action—the president can make a lot of final decisions on laws proposed by Congress. The president also has power over the armed forces (the army, marine corps, navy, air force, and coast guard).

SO PRESIDENTIAL

There was a three-week debate in Congress about how to address George Washington after his election, while planning his **inauguration** (when he was sworn into office). The Senate at the time proposed lofty titles like "His Highness, President of the United States and Protector of Their Liberties." The House of Representatives insisted that anything more than "President" would sound too powerful, like a monarch or **dictator**. It was the first big argument between the Senate and the House. In the end, the Senate gave in. The un-powerful sounding (at the time) title of "President" helped people feel more comfortable that this would not become a **dictatorship**.

TIME LIMITS

The president and VP get elected at the same time, and they serve together for four years. Until 1951, presidents could be in power for as long as they could win! However, this changed after Franklin Delano Roosevelt (FDR) served for 12 years. (See Amendment 22 on page 94.)

POWER CHECK

The president has a lot of clout, but is relatively unpowerful compared to a king, queen, or dictator. Checks and balances ensure that the president can't make major decisions without a lot of other people's approval.

PRESIDENT FAST FACTS

The president is:
★ the head of the military
★ the leader of the executive agencies, like the Department of the Treasury and the Department of Health and Human Services.

The president can:
★ pardon any person who has committed a federal crime
★ make treaties with foreign countries and appoint ambassadors, judges, and more (with the approval of the Senate).

The president must:
★ report to Congress about how the country is doing. The "State of the Union Address" is given every year and is televised and live-streamed across the world.

Q: How many presidents have served in the United States?

A. As of 2020, there have been 44 presidents. Donald Trump is the 45th, because Grover Cleveland was both the 22nd president and the 24th president! He was the only one who served for two non-consecutive terms.

WHAT ABOUT THE VICE PRESIDENT?

Can you name a vice president? The VP is second in command and takes over the presidency if the president is impeached or dies (see more on page 100). The VP is also head of the Senate, and votes if there's a tie.

WHAT DO YOU THINK ?

Dozens of other countries have followed the United States' example and call their elected leader "President." Do you think this title sounds powerful? What do you think would be a good title? Would you like to be president?

Article 2: President

★

NO ONE IS ABOVE THE LAW

The House of Representatives has the power to bring charges against the president for criminal or corrupt behavior. This is called impeachment, and it leads to a trial conducted by the Senate. If convicted (found guilty) by two-thirds of the Senate, the president can be removed from office.

Three presidents have been impeached. The 17th president, Andrew Johnson, was impeached in 1868, and the 42nd president, Bill Clinton, was in 1998. However, neither was removed from office. Richard Nixon, the 37th president, resigned in 1974 during an impeachment process. In December 2019, the 45th president, Donald Trump, was impeached. He was not removed from office.

WHERE ARE THE WOMEN?

Lots of women have tried, but so far there have been no female presidents of the United States. Yet! Here are some of the notable women who have run for president:

Victoria Woodhull

ran for president in 1872—almost 50 years before women had the right to vote in all states!

Margaret Chase Smith

was, in 1964, the first woman to run in the **primaries** of a major party.

Shirley Chisholm

was, in 1972, the first Black woman to seek a party's nomination.

Patsy Takemoto Mink

was the first Asian American to seek nomination by a major party, also in 1972.

Hillary Clinton

has run for president twice, in 2008 and 2016. She was the first woman nominated by a major party and the first to win the popular vote (see page 67 for more on the popular vote).

HOW A LAW IS MADE

Part 2

When a bill is agreed upon and has gone through the arduous arguing process in the Senate and the House, it goes to the president.

The president has two options:

1. The president signs it, and it becomes a law!

2. The president vetos it. Veto is a big NO. That's a lot of power.

But wait! A vetoed bill can still become a law. If two-thirds of the House agree, they can override the president. Checks and balances wins again!

FUN FACT!
KIDS IN THE WHITE HOUSE

Many children of past presidents lived in the White House over the years. John Tyler, the 10th president, had the most kids—15 in total!

FUN FACT!
A ZOO!

Two presidents were rumored to have had pet alligators in the White House: Herbert Hoover and John Quincy Adams. Calvin Coolidge had lots of animals too, including lion cubs! Many other presidents have had more cuddly pets like dogs and cats.

Q. How old do you need to be to become president?

A: The minimum age is 35. Historically, the youngest to be elected was the 35th president, JFK (he was 43), and the oldest was the 40th president, Ronald Reagan, who was elected at 73.

Two women have also been on the ballot for **VP** for major parties:

Geraldine Ferraro
in 1984

Sarah Palin
in 2008

A FEW FIRST LADIES AND THEIR CONTRIBUTIONS

Eleanor Roosevelt

was married to President Franklin Delano Roosevelt, and was the first lady from 1933 to 1945. She was a renowned humanitarian, feminist, and activist. She travelled widely and **advocated** for the rights of women, People of Color, and refugees.

Jackie Kennedy

was married to President John F. Kennedy and was the first lady from 1961 to 1963. She widely promoted the arts and hosted many performances of dance, theater, and music at the White House. She was also greatly admired as a style and fashion icon.

Michelle Obama

is married to President Barack Obama, and was the first Black first lady, from 2009 to 2017. In her role, she promoted healthy living, higher education, support for veterans, and education for girls around the world.

ARTICLE 3: JUDICIAL

Signed September 17, 1787. Ratified June 21, 1788. A part of Article 3 was later updated by the 11th Amendment.

★

"THE JUDICIAL POWER OF THE UNITED STATES, SHALL BE VESTED IN ONE SUPREME COURT, AND IN SUCH INFERIOR COURTS AS THE CONGRESS MAY FROM TIME TO TIME ORDAIN AND ESTABLISH. THE JUDGES, BOTH OF THE SUPREME AND INFERIOR COURTS, SHALL HOLD THEIR OFFICES DURING GOOD BEHAVIOUR, AND SHALL, AT STATED TIMES, RECEIVE FOR THEIR SERVICES, A COMPENSATION, WHICH SHALL NOT BE DIMINISHED DURING THEIR CONTINUANCE IN OFFICE."

Article 3 is about the third branch of government: judicial (the courts). This branch has the power to interpret laws and put them into action.

SUPREME COURT

The highest court in the land, made up of nine justices (judges) who are appointed by the president, with the Senate's approval.

INFERIOR COURTS

This means any courts other than the Supreme Court. Despite the slightly rude name, these courts are still very important!

JUDGES

They decide the verdict on cases in a court of law.

HOLD THEIR OFFICES DURING GOOD BEHAVIOR

Judges keep their jobs until they retire (as long as their behavior is good). This makes sure they are always impartial and would never make a decision based on fear of being fired.

COMPENSATION

Judges get paid. The amount they get paid can't be lowered at any point.

JUDICIAL FAST FACTS

U.S. Supreme Court

★ Includes **nine justices** who are appointed by the president (who needs the Senate's approval).

★ The Supreme Court helps us understand the Constitution, a document that can be (sometimes intentionally) vague. It's the courts' job to interpret the Constitution and fill in the details when needed. That's why we share Supreme Court cases in this book. They show how the Constitution is understood and used today.

Other courts

★ Lower federal courts in **every state**.

★ **Appellate courts:** where you can argue with the lower courts' decision, and sometimes have your case reach all the way to the Supreme Court.

AGREE TO DISAGREE

Different presidents from different parties appoint Supreme Court justices, and they serve for life (or as long as they want). This means that these justices often deeply disagree with one another—and that's by design. Take, for example, **Ruth Bader Ginsburg** and **Antonin Scalia**. They served on the Supreme Court together for more than 22 years and rarely agreed on controversial issues. Yet, they maintained a close friendship and always argued with a sense of humor. Here they are on a trip they took together to India in 1994.

SO JUDGEMENTAL

Judicial Review means the Supreme Court has the power to check up on the rest of government—Congress, the president and cabinet, and state governments—to make sure they are working in line with the Constitution.

WHAT DO YOU THINK

People who don't agree can still be friends and respect each other. Do you agree or disagree with that statement?

SONIA SOTOMAYOR

Sonia Sotomayor was born in NYC to parents from Puerto Rico. While she did not grow up with financial privilege, she had richness in her life through her family, community, and mentors.

Sotomayor wanted to be a judge from a young age, after watching shows on TV! She was a star student: she went to college at Princeton, where she received a big award, and then to Yale Law school. She worked hard as an attorney, and later as a law professor too. In 2009, President Obama nominated her to the Supreme Court, as our first Hispanic and Latina Supreme Court justice.

FUN FACT!
FRUITS OF THE VINE

Sometimes the Supreme Court, a serious set of people, has to make decisions on seemingly silly cases. For example, in 1893, the justices classified tomatoes and pickles as "Fruits of the Vine" (they're not a vegetable because of the seeds). However, they ruled that since everyone uses them as vegetables, they should be classified as such for trade purposes. This was helpful for farmers and produce sellers—and led to many years of confusion for the rest of us!

Q. There is just one president in U.S. history who was also a Supreme Court justice. Who was it?

A. William Howard Taft, the 27th president from 1909 to 1913. After his presidency, he became the 10th chief justice from 1921 to 1930.

ARTICLE 4: STATES

Signed September 17, 1787. Ratified June 21, 1788. A part of Article 4 was updated by the 13th Amendment.

★

Article 4 is all about the states: how they are created, how they're added to the Union, and how different states' laws work together. It also says it's the federal government's responsibility to protect the people from invasions (such as during a war) and not the responsibility of the states to defend themselves.

"FULL FAITH AND CREDIT SHALL BE GIVEN IN EACH STATE TO THE PUBLIC ACTS, RECORDS, AND JUDICIAL PROCEEDINGS OF EVERY OTHER STATE."

This means states must accept other states' laws when people travel around. For example, if someone is married in one state, their marriage must be recognized by any state they visit.

"NEW STATES MAY BE ADMITTED BY THE CONGRESS... BUT NO NEW STATE SHALL BE FORMED... WITHIN THE JURISDICTION OF ANY OTHER STATE."

Congress can add new states to the Union, but a state cannot be created inside another state. Also, Congress is allowed to sell off territories—land that is not a state, or inside a state.

"CITIZENS OF EACH STATE SHALL BE ENTITLED TO ALL PRIVILEGES AND IMMUNITIES OF CITIZENS IN THE SEVERAL STATES."

States must give non-residents the same treatment as residents, unless they are a fugitive (running from the law), in which case they must be returned to their home state. This section refers to slavery without mentioning it directly—by law, enslaved people seeking freedom were to be returned to slaveholders if they were found in another state. Although the enslavement of African people was hardly mentioned in the Constitution, it was silently woven between the lines.

"THE UNITED STATES SHALL GUARANTEE TO EVERY STATE IN THIS UNION A REPUBLICAN FORM OF GOVERNMENT, AND SHALL PROTECT EACH OF THEM AGAINST INVASION..."

It's not certain, but people think this means that every state must be run by representatives who the people have elected to represent them, not as a monarchy or any other form of government. And, every state is protected by the federal government from invasion or violent uprisings.

POWER CHECK

The seesaw of power between states and the federal government helps make sure neither becomes too powerful over the other.

Eureka!

Each state has its own official **flower, bird, and tree.** They also have slogans! California's slogan is "Eureka" because back in the Gold Rush (in the mid 1800s) when people discovered a lot of gold there, they would shout out "Eureka!" ("I have found it" in Greek.)

STATE FAST FACTS

★ The United States bought **Alaska** from Russia for $7.2 million in 1867.

★ **Washington, D.C.**, or the District of Columbia, is not a state. It's our nation's capital. To find out more about D.C. turn to page 96.

★ **Puerto Rico** is a territory, not a state. As of the writing of this book, there's a bill in Congress to make PR the 51st state.

CAN YOU NAME ALL 50 STATES?

Q: How many states were in the original United States?

A. There were 13 original states.

ARTICLE 5: AMENDING

Signed September 17, 1787. Ratified June 21, 1788.

★

"THE CONGRESS, WHENEVER TWO THIRDS OF BOTH HOUSES SHALL DEEM IT NECESSARY, SHALL PROPOSE AMENDMENTS TO THIS CONSTITUTION, OR, ON THE APPLICATION OF THE LEGISLATURES OF TWO THIRDS OF THE SEVERAL STATES, SHALL CALL A CONVENTION FOR PROPOSING AMENDMENTS..."

Article 5 tells us that the Constitution can be **amended** (changed), and explains how. The process is fairly simple. But don't let the simplicity fool you—it's very difficult to make an amendment. In order to amend the Constitution, many people with many different opinions need to agree. **Hello, debates!**

Q. In what year was the most recent amendment ratified?

A. Check page 104 to find out!

HOW DO WE AMEND THE CONSTITUTION?

It's complicated. Ready?

FIRST: An amendment is proposed. This can be done in two ways:

EITHER: Two-thirds of both the House of Representatives and the Senate come together to propose an amendment.

OR: Two-thirds of the states call a convention at which amendments are proposed (this method has never been used).

THEN: It's ratified. Again, this can be done in two ways:

EITHER: Three-quarters of state legislatures (Senate and House) agree and decide "yes" on the amendment.

OR: Three-quarters of the states agree and decide "yes" on the amendment at ratifying conventions. (Only one amendment, the 21st, was ratified in this way.)

PHEW!

No wonder the Constitution only has **27 amendments** of the 1100 that have been proposed!

DEBATE! THE CONSTITUTION

Consider the two viewpoints below. Think about them carefully or discuss them with a friend or family member. What do you think is the best course of action?

VIEWPOINT 1:

The Constitution is more relevant today than ever. We need to revisit it and reclaim it as the living document it was intended to be; one that can be interpreted in new ways and evolve as time passes.

VIEWPOINT 2:

The Constitution is old and flawed. It's too hard to amend, and we need to move on and make changes to the law and the government in other ways.

SOME AMENDMENTS THAT HAVE BEEN PROPOSED BUT NEVER RATIFIED WOULD:

★ Permit immigrants to become president (currently only American-born citizens can become president).

★ Set term limits for Congress (like the two-term limit we have for the president).

★ Change the country's name from the United States of America to the United States of Earth.

And many, many more!

THE EPIC EQUAL RIGHTS AMENDMENT

The Equal Rights Amendment (ERA) was designed to guarantee equal legal rights for American citizens regardless of sex. **Alice Paul** introduced the first version in Congress in December 1923. Since then, it has been ratified by different states over time. The most recent was Virginia in January, 2020. Will it ever be included in the Constitution? It is yet to be seen.

ARTICLE 6: DEBTS, SUPREMACY, OATHS, RELIGIOUS TESTS

Signed September 17, 1787. Ratified June 21, 1788.

★

"... THIS CONSTITUTION, AND THE LAWS OF THE UNITED STATES ... SHALL BE THE SUPREME LAW OF THE LAND; AND THE JUDGES IN EVERY STATE SHALL BE BOUND THEREBY, ANY THING IN THE CONSTITUTION OR LAWS OF ANY STATE TO THE CONTRARY NOTWITHSTANDING..."

Article 6 contains the **Supremacy Clause**, which lays out the agreement of the states to join together as one nation. States have their own laws, and the Constitution introduced federal laws for the whole nation. If state and federal laws conflict, this article says federal law is "supreme" over state.

MALCOLM X

"NO RELIGIOUS TEST SHALL EVER BE REQUIRED"

Elected officials are often sworn in to office by placing their hand on a Bible and promising to do their best. But forcing someone to do so would be a kind of religious test, and that's not allowed according to Article 6. In 2018, **Mariah Parker** was sworn in as an Athens-Clarke County commissioner while putting her hand over the autobiography of **Malcolm X**, an important Black Muslim activist and leader in the African American community in the 1960s.

BOTH PARTS OF THE COUNTRY
ARE VITAL AND NEED BALANCING.

UNITED

The federal government has some power over states. For example, the FDA (Food and Drug Administration) makes laws about food and drugs that all states need to abide by. Federal law is "supreme" over state law. If there's a disagreement, the courts get involved.

STATES

The states were here first! They have their own governments and elections, and they make laws that affect our day-to-day lives. Americans in different states have different laws regarding healthcare, property, and criminal activity. Gun control laws are also different from state to state.

ARTICLE 7: RATIFICATION

Signed September 17, 1787. Ratified June 21, 1788.

★

"THE RATIFICATION OF THE CONVENTIONS OF NINE STATES, SHALL BE SUFFICIENT FOR THE ESTABLISHMENT OF THIS CONSTITUTION BETWEEN THE STATES SO RATIFYING THE SAME..."

The final article of the original Constitution outlines what needs to happen for the Constitution to become official—in short, it needed to be signed and agreed to by nine states: two-thirds majority of the thirteen original states!

THE FRAMERS WERE REBELS

When the Constitution was written, James Madison and Alexander Hamilton (two of the main writers) were both in their 30s and half of the other signers were under the age of 45. That's pretty young! When we see pictures of them in their wigs and old-fashioned clothes, it's hard to imagine that they were young revolutionaries with big, edgy ideas compared to most other white land-owning men. America had just become free from England, and they were taking a huge risk in forming this new government—if it didn't work and they ended up back under British rule, they'd be in BIG trouble. Many thought they were crazy to do this, but it was an exciting time and a bold move.

THE FRAMERS WERE FLAWED

Although rebels in their own right, the **framers** were also deeply flawed. Many of the **Founding Fathers**, as they are sometimes called, recognized in theory that slavery was inhumane, immoral, and in direct contradiction with their ideal of "liberty." But their focus on profit over people stopped them from ending it. And where was the freedom for women and Native Americans, who could not vote? We'll talk about this more when we come to the 19th Amendment (see page 86).

WHITEWASHING HISTORY

Have you ever noticed a lot of American history books talk more about white men than Native Americans, People of Color, or women? Our history is often told from a white patriarchal perspective, and we tend to learn just one side of many stories. This is changing today. Look in your school books and see if they are teaching more than one perspective.

Iroquois chief Canasatego was a spokesman for the Iroquois Confederacy, a union of six Native American nations in what became Pennsylvania. He attended conferences with the framers as a representative of his people, and some historians say he advised the framers on how to form a union based on the example of the Iroquois Confederacy. He said, "We heartily recommend Union and a Good Agreement between you our Brethren. Never disagree, but preserve a strict Friendship for one another, and thereby you as well as we will become the Stronger."

WHO ARE THESE GUYS?
Here are some of the framers who signed the Constitution.

Alexander Hamilton
was a statesman, politician, legal scholar, military commander, lawyer, banker, and economist. He also founded the nation's financial system, the Federalist Party.

Benjamin Franklin
was an inventor, scientist, politician, and diplomat. You may have heard stories of him flying a kite in a storm! He also helped write the Constitution and negotiated the 1783 Treaty of Paris ending the Revolutionary War.

George Washington
led the Colonial revolutionary army to victory over the British and became the 1st president of the United States.

James Madison
helped write the Constitution and was the 4th president of the United States.

New York

Vermont

Massachusetts

Pennsylvania

Connecticut

Rhode Island

Maryland

New Jersey

Delaware

Virginia

North Carolina

South Carolina

Georgia

Q. Which of the original 13 states did not send a delegate to the Constitutional Convention?

A. Rhode Island. They were also the last state to ratify the Constitution, because they were worried about the federal government getting too strong. They also didn't like that the Constitution did not protect religious freedoms (this only came later). For this, they earned the nickname "Rogue Island."

Part 2:
THE BILL OF RIGHTS

WHAT EXACTLY IS THE BILL OF RIGHTS?

Remember how Article 5 (page 28) says that the Constitution can be amended? Well, the framers added the **first ten amendments** right away. Together they are called "**The Bill of Rights**." The Bill of Rights was written in **1789** and ratified in **1791**, very soon after the Constitution, due to high demand. In fact, several framers did not sign the original Constitution because it was lacking a Bill of Rights! Its purpose is to protect the people from the government. But wait, the government IS the people, right? We elect officials to their positions. So why do we need protection?

Some people think human nature can lead to abuse of power. The men who wrote the Constitution thought about this a lot. What if you were elected to a very powerful position? Would you use your power to outlaw vegetables and bedtime? Or advocate for a healthier and less-sleepy country? Even when we elect great people, the Bill of Rights is supposed to ensure that our unconditional rights cannot be taken away. They are meant to protect our rights from ever being violated by a government getting too powerful.

> *They are the values that define us as a people, the ideals that challenge us to perfect our union, and the liberties that generations of Americans have fought to preserve at home and abroad."*

PRESIDENT BARACK OBAMA
Speech on Race, 2008

Q. When was the Bill of Rights added to the Constitution?

A. The 10 Amendments included in the Bill of Rights were all ratified in 1791, three years after the ratification of the original Constitution in 1788.

DID YOU KNOW?

The U.S. Bill of Rights is a respected document in the world. Other countries have modelled their own versions inspired by ours.

DEBATE! THE BILL OF RIGHTS

Consider the two viewpoints below. Think about them carefully or discuss them with a friend or family member. What do you think about each statement?

VIEWPOINT 1:

The Bill of Rights holds a high standard that we can aspire to. It allows us to have continuous forward movement towards equality—something we still don't have today in the U.S.

VIEWPOINT 2:

The Bill of Rights is all about human rights, yet it didn't count Native Americans as citizens. Also, slavery was still legal when it was written! This is total hypocrisy and the Bill of Rights is too flawed and biased to ever truly protect the people.

1ST AMENDMENT

Passed by Congress September 25, 1789. Ratified December 15, 1791.

★

FREEDOM OF RELIGION, SPEECH, PRESS, ASSEMBLY, PETITIONS

"CONGRESS SHALL MAKE NO LAW RESPECTING AN ESTABLISHMENT OF RELIGION, OR PROHIBITING THE FREE EXERCISE THEREOF; OR ABRIDGING THE FREEDOM OF SPEECH, OR OF THE PRESS; OR THE RIGHT OF THE PEOPLE PEACEABLY TO ASSEMBLE, AND TO PETITION THE GOVERNMENT FOR A REDRESS OF GRIEVANCES."

The first amendment outlines several basic and important freedoms that everyone in the U.S. has the right to. These include freedom of religion, speech, and the press, the right to **assemble** and the right to petition the government. They're some of the most argued and debated rights in the whole Constitution!

FREEDOM OF RELIGION

This means that anyone may practice whichever religion they choose, and no one can be made to practice a religion either. This is called **"Separation of Church and State"** —the government should be neutral and not interfere with or promote religion in any way.

THE RIGHT TO PETITION

We can **speak up** to the government about anything we don't like. This is the first step in any change that happens! You can even write to the president directly. Turn to page 109 to find out how to do this. What will you write?

FREEDOM OF SPEECH AND OF THE PRESS

In some countries, writers and reporters can be punished or even killed for writing about certain topics. But in the U.S., the 1st Amendment protects our right to the freedom of speech. We will not be silenced. We have the right within the law to say and publish whatever we want!

THE RIGHT OF THE PEOPLE PEACEABLY TO ASSEMBLE

Under the 1st Amendment, we can gather together to do whatever we like, as long as it's peaceful. We can protest something we don't like, or campaign for a candidate we want to elect.

1st Amendment

★

How does the 1st Amendment relate to us in our everyday lives? What does it mean to exercise these rights? Take a look at the following cases and stories to understand the wider context of the 1st Amendment and how we can all make sure we protect and uphold it.

THE RIGHT TO WRITE (AND READ!)

When the *Wonder Woman* comic book came out in 1942, it was banned! Among other complaints, critics felt the superhero was not "sufficiently dressed." This is called **censorship**, and it goes against the Constitution. Even today, censorship can happen and people have to stand up for the right to **freedom of the press**.

DIFFERENT OPINIONS

Sometimes **freedom of speech** means that we are exposed to opinions different from our own, or even to negative content that makes us feel uncomfortable. The Constitution doesn't say we have the right to be comfortable and it's important for everyone to have their say. Why do you think it might be important to hear different opinions?

ON THE INTERNET

What is considered offensive can seem to have different rules in real life and online. The Supreme Court generally rules in favor of people using curse words in the street as long as they're not creating any danger. What about when they are used online? "One man's vulgarity is another's lyric," one judge famously noted. We are just beginning to explore and debate censorship and freedom of speech online. **What do you think about this?**

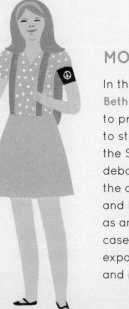

MORE THAN WORDS

In the mid 1960s, a girl named Mary Beth Tinker wore a black armband to protest a war. Her school tried to stop her, and her case went to the Supreme Court. After much debate, they decided that wearing the armband was within her rights and Mary Beth continued to wear it as an act of protest. Because of her case, the right to free speech was expanded to include symbols, music, and more.

GOD COMES IN ALL SHAPES AND SIZES

The government can't establish an "official" religion for the country. This is important, because the freedom to practice religion (or not) is a basic right. In other parts of the world, people can get in trouble if they don't practice the religion of their government.

Here are just a few of the religions practiced freely in the U.S.:

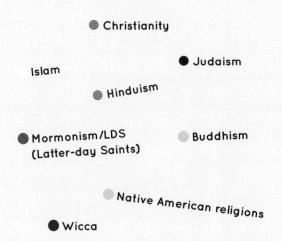

- Christianity
- Judaism
- Islam
- Hinduism
- Mormonism/LDS (Latter-day Saints)
- Buddhism
- Native American religions
- Wicca

Many people are **agnostic**, which means they neither believe nor disbelieve in God; they feel that any god is unknowable. Others are **atheists**, which means they don't believe in a god.

SPEAKING UP AT SCHOOL

In 1989 a principal of a school in Rhode Island invited a rabbi to give a prayer at the school's graduation ceremony. **Deborah Weisman**, a student at the time, knew that having a prayer at graduation was against the Constitution. She stood up to her principal and said so. She then took her case to the Supreme Court, who decided she was right! Now, schools can't have prayers at graduation, and Deborah's case led the way for others to take action against prayers in school.

However, kids are still saying "under God" in the pledge of allegiance across the country every day. What's more, the Christian religion is present in a lot of public institutions like schools and political offices, even though **Separation of Church and State** says it shouldn't be. The more people who speak up and exercise their rights, the more change we can expect to see.

RIGHTS V. RIGHTS?

In 2012 two men in Colorado placed an order for a wedding cake at their local bakery. But the baker refused to make the cake because he was against marriage between people of the same sex, for religious reasons. The Supreme Court decided that the baker's religious freedom outweighed the couple's right to equal treatment. Sometimes different rights seem to contradict each other, and the court must decide. This case is still controversial and hotly debated.

Welcome to the U.S.A., where we have more gun freedom AND more gun deaths than anywhere else in the world.

2ND AMENDMENT

Passed by Congress September 25, 1789. Ratified December 15, 1791.

━━━━━━━━━━━━━━━━━★━━━━━━━━━━━━━━━━━

ARMS

"A WELL REGULATED MILITIA, BEING NECESSARY TO THE SECURITY OF A FREE STATE, THE RIGHT OF THE PEOPLE TO KEEP AND BEAR ARMS, SHALL NOT BE INFRINGED."

The 2nd Amendment is all about guns, and was considered irrelevant for many years. Then everything changed. This amendment is one of the most difficult to interpret because it can be (and is) interpreted in different ways.

One thing we know for sure is that at the time it was written, people needed to be able to form a militia (a military force of non-military people in a time of need), potentially to fight foreign troops, or to protect against a government that was becoming overly repressive. Later, it was interpreted differently to be about regular people having guns.

DID YOU KNOW?

Americans have the most guns per person in the world. Around 4 out of every 10 people either own a gun or live in a home with guns.

Some say, the second amendment, is hard, to interpret, with all those, commas!

2ⁿᵈ Amendment

★

DID YOU KNOW?

The Black Panthers ran a free breakfast program for kids that inspired the government to provide free meals to students, which is still in practice today.

INTERPRETING THE CONSTITUTION:
THE RIGHT TO FORM A MILITIA

The **Black Panthers** were a revolutionary Black organization in the United States dedicated to socialist ideas. They used the 2nd Amendment to take a stand for their rights and defend their communities from a corrupt and violent police force, by monitoring police activity in armed groups. The Constitution gave them a framework for their legal right to form a militia.

> **"** *Any politicians being funded by the NRA ... on these people, we call BS.* **"**

EMMA GONZÁLEZ

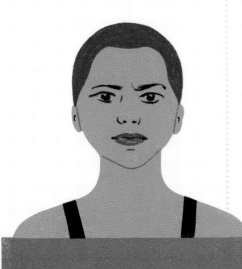

"WE ARE GOING TO BE THE KIDS YOU READ ABOUT IN TEXTBOOKS."

INTERPRETING THE CONSTITUTION:
THE RIGHT TO BEAR ARMS

The **NRA** (National Rifle Association) was once a sporting club and has changed a lot over the years. The version we know today is a huge political force that lobbies aggressively for gun owners' rights. The NRA pulled the words "the right to bear arms" from the Constitution to use as a marketing slogan, but those words alone have a different meaning out of context. Even so, in 2008, the Supreme Court passed legislation declaring that the "right to bear arms" extends to personal firearms. The original meaning of the amendment had now completely changed.

GUNS TODAY

Today, gun control activists fight for stronger legislation in the aftermath of mass shootings in schools, as the debate about the 2nd amendment goes on.

KIDS TAKING ACTION

Emma González gave a viral speech against gun violence and organized the "March for Our Lives" after 17 people were killed in her high school in a 2018 shooting in Parkland, Florida.

DEBATE!
THE BIG GUN DEBATE

Consider the two viewpoints below. Think about them carefully or discuss them with a friend or family member.

What do you think about each statement?

VIEWPOINT 1:

Guns should be highly controlled and carried only by police.

VIEWPOINT 2:

All people have the right to carry guns to defend themselves.

3RD AMENDMENT

Passed by Congress September 25, 1789. Ratified December 15, 1791.

★

QUARTERING OF SOLDIERS

This amendment was very specific to the time when it was written and has never been needed for its original purpose!

"NO SOLDIER SHALL, IN TIME OF PEACE BE QUARTERED IN ANY HOUSE, WITHOUT THE CONSENT OF THE OWNER, NOR IN TIME OF WAR, BUT IN A MANNER TO BE PRESCRIBED BY LAW."

THE REDCOATS BARGED RIGHT IN

During the time leading up to the United States gaining independence from Britain, British soldiers, who were known as the Redcoats (guess why!) assumed the right to stay in people's homes. People were not happy about these uninvited guests barging in and helping themselves to food and shelter. It was so horrific that some framers insisted putting this into the Constitution just in case it came up again. Fortunately, the war ended and it wasn't an issue.

WHAT'S NEXT?

It's good to know that it's written in law that no one can forcibly camp out in our homes. But privacy is increasingly a public issue today. Cameras are everywhere, wireless speakers are listening, and internet companies know everything about us. Can you imagine the 3rd Amendment making a comeback?

4TH AMENDMENT

Passed by Congress September 25, 1789. Ratified December 15, 1791.

★

SEARCH AND SEIZURE

"THE RIGHT OF THE PEOPLE TO BE SECURE IN THEIR PERSONS, HOUSES, PAPERS, AND EFFECTS, AGAINST UNREASONABLE SEARCHES AND SEIZURES, SHALL NOT BE VIOLATED, AND NO WARRANTS SHALL ISSUE, BUT UPON PROBABLE CAUSE..."

The 4th Amendment states that no one can search or take your stuff or put you in prison unless you've broken the law or are suspected of breaking the law—kind of.

WARRANT

This is a paper given to the police by a judge or lawmaker permitting them to search someone's stuff. It says there's a good reason to believe that this person broke the law. For example, if someone is suspected of murder, the police can get a warrant to search their house for a weapon or other evidence.

PROBABLE CAUSE

This is the legal name for "good reason." Sometimes probable cause can be decided in the moment by a police officer when there isn't time to get a warrant—for example, if they see someone who matches the description of a bank robber.

There's a warrant out for this guy's arrest.

DON'T BE NOSY, GOVERNMENT

Like all the amendments in the Bill of Rights, this one's designed to protect our rights. If you haven't broken the law, the government has to leave you alone.

MODERN CONCERNS

When the Constitution was written, we didn't have email or cellphones. We're still figuring out how the law should affect us now—can the police search your phone? Or your private social-media account?

WHAT ABOUT KIDS' RIGHTS?

Your parents don't need a warrant to look through your phone. And in schools, the responsibility to protect kids outweighs their right to privacy. For example, random searches for weapons or drugs are allowed in schools. When the Constitution was written, kids were basically considered the property of their parents. *No fair!*

CONTROVERSY IN NYC

"Stop and Frisk" is the practice of police randomly stopping people and patting them down for weapons or drugs. Young Black and Latino men are targeted far more than other people. This is **demeaning** and fails to protect their basic rights. After a big lawsuit with the **New York Civil Liberties Union**, the number of Stop and Frisks in NYC went down from 700,000 in 2011 to about 12,000 in 2017.

RACIAL PROFILING

Black and brown people are stopped, searched and questioned by police far more often than white people in America, even though the law is supposed to protect everyone equally. It's called racial profiling and it's discriminatory—police officers aren't supposed to stop someone based on the way they look, but they do anyway because of ingrained bias and prejudice.

5TH AMENDMENT

Passed by Congress September 25, 1789. Ratified December 15, 1791.

★

GRAND JURY, DOUBLE JEOPARDY, SELF-INCRIMINATION, DUE PROCESS

The 5th Amendment lays out some very powerful and specific rights that we all have and can use if we are accused of a crime. The 5th (and 6th) Amendments are about criminal justice.

WHAT IS JUSTICE?

Justice means morally right and fair behavior or treatment.

Criminal justice means delivery of justice to those who have committed crimes.

Justice is a tricky word, because what's "morally right and fair" depends on what you believe. Justice can look different depending on your own viewpoint. When an innocent person is accused of a crime and goes free, that's justice! When a guilty person goes to jail, is that justice too?

THE RIGHT TO AN ATTORNEY

Anyone accused of a crime has the right to go through the same judicial process as anyone else. That includes having an attorney, or lawyer—a professional who has studied the law and represents them, their rights, and their best interest through the process. Some lawyers are really expensive and not everyone can afford one. In that case, the court must provide the person on trial with legal representation (see page 52).

Judge

Witness

Plaintiff

Attorney

INNOCENT UNTIL PROVEN GUILTY

If the Bill of Rights could talk, it might say:
"It's better to let a guilty person go free than to unfairly punish an innocent person by mistake." This is not just about being morally right, it's also supposed to ensure freedom from government oppression. If innocent people live in fear of being randomly imprisoned, we are not free.

Unfortunately, many people do live in fear—the criminal justice system in the U.S. is flawed, because of systemic racism and bias that's embedded in the system. The criminal justice system needs to be improved so that equality prevails.

Q. Which state does not have its own police force?

A. Unlike every other state, Hawaii does not have a state police force. Each of the counties in Hawaii has its own police force!

Jury

5th Amendment

★

"NO PERSON SHALL BE HELD TO ANSWER FOR A CAPITAL, OR OTHERWISE INFAMOUS CRIME, UNLESS ON A PRESENTMENT OR INDICTMENT OF A GRAND JURY ... NOR SHALL ANY PERSON BE SUBJECT FOR THE SAME OFFENSES TO BE TWICE PUT IN JEOPARDY OF LIFE OR LIMB; NOR SHALL BE COMPELLED IN ANY CRIMINAL CASE TO BE A WITNESS AGAINST HIMSELF, NOR BE DEPRIVED OF LIFE, LIBERTY, OR PROPERTY, WITHOUT DUE PROCESS OF LAW..."

This amendment is very practical! Here are some more rights that protect people on trial. It's also important to mention that although the 5th Amendment protects individuals, it does NOT protect businesses or corporations.

CAPITAL CRIME

This means a "serious" crime, such as murder, which in some states is punishable by death.

INFAMOUS CRIME

This is a crime involving dishonesty, such as fraud (cheating or deceiving people for gain).

INDICTMENT

If someone is accused of a serious crime like murder, a group of people called a Grand Jury must first discuss and decide that the accusation is valid (legally acceptable). Then they make a formal charge called an indictment.

BE TWICE PUT IN JEOPARDY

Often called double jeopardy this means that a person can't be prosecuted (accused and made to go through the court system) for the same offense twice.

WITNESS AGAINST HIMSELF

A person can't be made to incriminate themselves—made to say something that might indicate their own guilt. Why do you think this is important?

DUE PROCESS

This means fair treatment through the judicial system. It's the only phrase that appears twice in the Constitution; here and in the 14th Amendment (see page 72).

THE RIGHT TO KNOW OUR RIGHTS

In the mid-1960s, **Ernesto Miranda** was convicted of a crime, but his lawyer felt it wasn't fair that he didn't even know his rights when he was arrested. What good are rights if people don't know what they are?

Because of his case, a law was made that police must read the following when arresting someone, now known as their **"Miranda Rights"**:

"You have the right to remain silent. Anything you say can and will be used against you in a court of law. You have the right to an attorney. If you cannot afford an attorney, one will be provided for you."

PLEADING THE 5TH

When people are on trial, they are usually pretty stressed out regardless of whether or not they're guilty. The 5th Amendment says you can't be made to incriminate yourself (which means to give evidence that implies your own guilt). This protects us from being intimidated into giving a false confession. When someone says, "I plead the 5th," it means they choose not to talk about their involvement (or not) in the crime.

WHAT DO YOU THINK?

Why do you think it's important to know your rights? We hope when you finish this book, you'll know a lot more about your constitutional rights.

6TH AMENDMENT

Passed by Congress September 25, 1789. Ratified December 15, 1791.

★

RIGHTS OF ACCUSED IN CRIMINAL PROSECUTIONS

The Power of an Individual

THE RIGHT TO A LAWYER

Court case of *Gideon v. Wainwright* (1963)

Clarence Earl Gideon was charged with a crime, and the court did not appoint him a lawyer when he requested one. He felt this breached his rights. He studied the Constitution and fought for his rights while in prison. His case went to the Supreme Court where they decided that anyone who can't afford a lawyer must be given a lawyer by the government. They used the 6th and the 14th Amendments to make this argument.

> "IN ALL CRIMINAL PROSECUTIONS, THE ACCUSED SHALL ENJOY THE RIGHT TO A SPEEDY AND PUBLIC TRIAL, BY AN IMPARTIAL JURY ... TO BE CONFRONTED WITH THE WITNESSES AGAINST HIM; TO HAVE COMPULSORY PROCESS FOR OBTAINING WITNESSES IN HIS FAVOR, AND TO HAVE THE ASSISTANCE OF COUNSEL FOR HIS DEFENCE."

The 6th Amendment outlines a person's rights when they are accused of a crime. It goes on to to talk about the court process.

A SPEEDY AND PUBLIC TRIAL

What does a speedy trial mean? Some people wait a long time for trial—and that's not fair, because sometimes they wait in prison even when they might be innocent.

A public trial means anyone can come watch it in court. It holds the court accountable to do things fairly. Sometimes this, combined with the freedom of the press, gets tricky because cases involving famous people are so public. Sometimes lots of press can even affect the verdict!

WITNESSES AGAINST HIM

Second, every person on trial has the right to see and hear the opposing witnesses (people who think they are guilty), and ask them questions.

WITNESSES IN HIS FAVOR

Third, the person has the right to call in a witness (someone who can vouch for their innocence) by sending them something called a subpoena, requiring them to show up in court.

AN IMPARTIAL JURY

First, the accused person has the right to a jury trial, which means they have the right to go to court, have a judge, and have a jury (more about this on the next page). During the trial, the jury looks at the evidence, listens to the story, and decides if the person is guilty or not.

ASSISTANCE OF COUNSEL

And finally, every person has the right to counsel: to be represented by a lawyer who understands the process and can help them make their case. Usually, the lawyer questions the witnesses in court.

WHAT DO YOU THINK ?

Do you think communication is more effective in person than, say, over text? When someone is on trial, they have the right to question witnesses face to face in the courtroom.

7TH AMENDMENT

Passed by Congress September 25, 1789. Ratified December 15, 1791.

★

JURY TRIAL

"IN SUITS AT COMMON LAW, WHERE THE VALUE IN CONTROVERSY SHALL EXCEED TWENTY DOLLARS*, THE RIGHT OF TRIAL BY JURY SHALL BE PRESERVED, AND NO FACT TRIED BY A JURY, SHALL BE OTHERWISE RE-EXAMINED IN ANY COURT OF THE UNITED STATES, THAN ACCORDING TO THE RULES OF THE COMMON LAW."

The 7th Amendment extends the right of a jury trial to civil (non-criminal) cases in federal courts.

The jury must unanimously decide the verdict.
That means they all have to agree.

WHAT IS A CIVIL CASE?

Imagine a doctor makes a mistake during an operation. That can happen—it's not illegal. It just means that they made a mistake or did their job badly. But, does that patient (who just had surgery on the wrong knee, for example) deserve justice? Should the hospital be responsible for the mistake? Situations like this can become **civil** cases.

A CIVIL CASE COULD BE ABOUT:

* ★ property
* ★ divorce, child custody, child support
* ★ real-estate disputes
* ★ personal injury (getting hurt at work or in a public place)
* ★ medical malpractice (when a doctor makes a mistake).

✳ **$20** from the original amendment has gone up to about **$75,000** today for federal cases and varies across states. This "value in controversy" is the amount of money being claimed. For example, a patient may wish to claim **$500,000** for the inconvenience and trauma of having the wrong knee operated on.

WHAT IS A JURY?

A jury is a group of 6–12 people chosen to listen to a court case, and unanimously decide the verdict: guilty or not guilty in criminal cases, or in favor of the plaintiff or the defendant in civil cases.

Once the jury decides, the judge gives the sentence (punishment) if the verdict is guilty or in favor of the plaintiff.

Anyone 18 and older can serve on a jury—you may too one day! The courts summon people to "jury duty" by sending a letter in the mail.

The jury is supposed to represent the real population. However, juries have not always done so. Women weren't required on juries in all states until 1974.

The *Hernandez v. Texas* Supreme Court case in 1954 prohibits racial discrimination in jury selection. This case led us to *Brown v. the Board of Education* (see page 74).

Q. What state was the first to allow women on the jury?

A. Utah allowed women to sit on the jury as early as 1898!

8TH AMENDMENT

Passed by Congress September 25, 1789. Ratified December 15, 1791.

★

PROTECTING AGAINST EXCESSIVE BAIL, CRUEL AND UNUSUAL PUNISHMENT

"EXCESSIVE BAIL SHALL NOT BE REQUIRED, NOR EXCESSIVE FINES IMPOSED, NOR CRUEL AND UNUSUAL PUNISHMENTS INFLICTED."

JAIL

Prisons are overcrowded today, yet sentencing is growing
harsher. "Three strikes you're out," is a law in some states that says you get
a life sentence if you come back to jail three times.

The 8th Amendment is about what happens in the next steps of the justice system, and when someone is found guilty. What are our rights when we've been convicted of a crime?

BAIL

This means to release an accused person waiting for their trial. It also refers to money they have to pay to ensure they'll return (they get the money back when they show up for trial). But what if someone doesn't have enough money for bail? Sometimes they have to stay in a prison cell when they haven't been proven guilty. Does that seem fair?

CRUEL AND UNUSUAL PUNISHMENT

As society evolves, what is deemed "cruel and unusual" changes a lot. For example, many schools used to use corporal punishment (beating) on kids as discipline. For the most part, this has changed over time and is now seen as a cruel and inhumane act.

In the old days, people accused of crimes would be put in "the stocks" like in this picture, in the middle of town for all to see. Cruel, or unusual?

RACISM, DISCRIMINATION AT EVERY ANGLE

The prison system today, sometimes called the **Prison Industrial Complex**, is rife with discrimination and racism. Black people and People of Color outnumber white people in prison. This goes back to the time when slavery was abolished, and basically continued under a different name: prison. That concept is alive and well today, as the system is stacked against People of Color. According to the NAACP (National Association for the Advancement of Colored People):

★ Black folks are incarcerated (put into jail) at more than five times the rate of white people.

★ Black women are imprisoned two times more than white women.

★ Black children make up 35% of kids arrested in the U.S.

DEATH PENALTY

In the U.S., people convicted of really bad crimes such as murder can end up getting **sentenced to death**. Some people think this is fair and just, while others believe it is "cruel and unusual"—and just plain wrong. It is a fierce debate that is still ongoing.

In modern criminal investigations, the suspect's DNA is compared to the DNA evidence found at a crime scene. DNA testing is freeing many innocent people from **death row** (the "line" of people awaiting their death sentence in prison)— people who would have otherwise been killed for a crime they didn't commit. Sentencing an innocent person to death is one of the worst things the Bill of Rights could imagine. Would you get rid of the death penalty? Why or why not?

Q. How many states have the death penalty?

A. 29 states do! But very few use it regularly and 21 have banned it completely, including Hawaii, Alaska, and Vermont. The first state to ban it was Michigan in 1846, for all crimes except for treason.

WHAT DO YOU THINK ?

What rights do you think we should have that aren't listed in the Constitution?

List

○ Free speech

○ Freedom of the press

○ Freedom of religion

○ Right to a jury

○ Equal rights

○ Voting rights

○ Access to Education

○ Freedo

○ Free to choos

○ Equality at work

○ Equal pay

○ The right to eat pickles

○ to healthcare

Access to t

Freedom of M

9TH AMENDMENT

Passed by Congress September 25, 1789. Ratified December 15, 1791.

★

NON-ENUMERATED RIGHTS

"THE ENUMERATION IN THE CONSTITUTION, OF CERTAIN RIGHTS, SHALL NOT BE CONSTRUED TO DENY OR DISPARAGE OTHERS RETAINED BY THE PEOPLE."

The 9th Amendment is all about something called "Non-Enumerated Rights." Some people feared if we listed some of our rights, then only those rights would be protected. So this amendment covers "everything else". The 9th Amendment means that the government can't use the Constitution to deny us other rights not listed here. But what are they?

ENUMERATION

Enumerated rights are the ones listed so far.

THE RIGHT TO PRIVACY

Many people say that the right to privacy is an important one that the Constitution doesn't list. The case of *Roe v. Wade* in 1973 was all about whether or not a woman has the right to decide, privately with her doctor, to keep or end a pregnancy. The Constitution does not specifically say that a woman has to be a mother if she gets pregnant. Many people think it should say that, and this is a topic fiercely debated in America and other parts of the world. In *Roe v. Wade*, the judges used the 9th Amendment (as well as the 14th and others) to say that a woman does have the right to decide whether or not to keep a pregnancy.

10TH AMENDMENT

Passed by Congress September 25, 1789. Ratified December 15, 1791.

★

RIGHTS RESERVED TO STATES

"THE POWERS NOT DELEGATED TO THE UNITED STATES BY THE CONSTITUTION, NOR PROHIBITED BY IT TO THE STATES, ARE RESERVED TO THE STATES RESPECTIVELY, OR TO THE PEOPLE."

The 10th Amendment says the federal government only has the powers listed in the Constitution. All other unlisted powers are automatically **delegated** to the states.

The 10th Amendment can be difficult to interpret. Mostly, it means that the states are in charge of more local things, like transportation, schools, roads, and hospitals. The balance of power between the federal and state governments is questioned, debated, and examined year after year.

FEDERAL V. STATE FAST FACTS

Below is a list of some of the different things that federal and state governments are in charge of.

Some federal powers are:
* being in charge of the military and declaring war
* collecting federal taxes
* regulating commerce (business) between the states
* everything to do with money.

Some state powers are:
* traffic laws
* collecting local taxes
* issuing drivers' licenses
* holding elections
* building and maintaining roads and schools
* police and fire departments
* local business laws.

WHAT IF?

What if a state is doing something that goes against the ideals of the Constitution—but it's within their rights? Sometimes federal and state law can conflict with one another. We've seen the "Supremacy Clause" on page 31, which says that federal law trumps state law. However, this amendment shows that it's not always that simple, and that states have power too.

If there is a gap in federal law, or if a state law gives more rights to citizens than federal law has to offer, state law wins. For example, federal law doesn't always protect LGBTQAI+ rights, but some states do. The bottom line is, when federal and state laws come into conflict, the courts get involved and everyone argues until there's a resolution.

MONEY INCENTIVE

The federal government gives funding (money) to the states for various things, such as schools and roads. Sometimes they use this money as an incentive to get states to do things their way. *Does that seem right?*

A. New Hampshire, since 1945.

STATES' RIGHTS

States are so different from each other! Some are very densely populated, while others have thousands of miles of countryside. There are big cultural differences across different states too. It makes sense that states need their own laws and their own individual governments.

However, sometimes people bring up "states' rights" to argue that they shouldn't have to follow a federal law. It gets really controversial around gun control, for example. It's up to the Supreme Court to figure out what to do when the two are in conflict.

Part 3:
THE REST OF THE AMENDMENTS

The following pages contain all the rest of the amendments from the **11th Amendment right up to the most recent, the 27th Amendment.** Many of the amendments that have been made since the Bill of Rights have been attempts to correct discrimination previously unaddressed in the Constitution, including:

* gender discrimination
* race discrimination
* age discrimination.

Each of these amendments was ratified at a different time as We the People, in government and the courts, continued to evolve our democracy to make sure our rights are protected, and that justice is for all.

Q. How many times does the word "democracy" appear in the Constitution?

A. Zero! In legal terms, the United States is actually a republic, or a "representative" democracy. This means that most decisions are made by elected officials, and NOT directly by the people. A "pure" democracy is the rule of the majority, which can ultimately vote against freedoms. The U.S. is governed by the Constitution, NOT the majority, which ensures basic rights and freedoms to all citizens.

11TH AMENDMENT

Passed by Congress March 4, 1794. Ratified February 7, 1795. The 11th Amendment updated part of Article 3, Section 2.

★

SUITS AGAINST A STATE

"THE JUDICIAL POWER OF THE UNITED STATES SHALL NOT BE CONSTRUED TO EXTEND TO ANY SUIT… AGAINST ONE OF THE UNITED STATES BY CITIZENS OF ANOTHER STATE…"

According to the 11th Amendment, the states are **protected** from lawsuits brought against them by citizens of other states or foreign countries. The federal courts are simply not allowed to hear cases brought by private citizens against the states.

STATES VS. FEDERAL

The 11th Amendment is another example of the **push and pull between federal power and state power**. (See more in the 10th Amendment, page 60.) The question comes up again and again in the Constitution: are the states sovereign, which means totally legally independent?

According to the 11th Amendment, we see that states do have some **independence**. Federal government has limited power over them. It can't hear cases against them by private citizens, giving the states a protective shield and leaves some power in their hands. It's not total power though! In some cases, Congress can take away the states' **immunity**.

WHAT DO YOU THINK

Some amendments add something new to the Constitution, and others make a change to existing text. Either way, each one has to be added in order. The Constitution states that nothing can be deleted or removed from the original. Why do you think that's important?

12TH AMENDMENT

Passed by Congress December 9, 1803. Ratified June 15, 1804. Updated a part of Article 2, Section 1. Later, a part of the 12th Amendment was changed by the 20th Amendment.

★

ELECTION OF PRESIDENT AND VICE-PRESIDENT

"THE ELECTORS SHALL MEET IN THEIR RESPECTIVE STATES AND VOTE BY BALLOT FOR PRESIDENT AND VICE-PRESIDENT..."

According to the 12th Amendment, the Electoral College (people from every state that vote for the president) vote for one person to be the president, and for a different person to be the vice president. Sounds obvious, right? It wasn't always so!

CHECKLIST: CAN YOU BE ELECTED PRESIDENT?

☐ You are over 35 years old.

☐ You were born in the U.S.

☐ You have lived in the U.S. for 14 years.

ELECTIONS, REVISITED

The 12th Amendment solved a problem with elections. According to Article 2, electors from every state used to vote for two people who they thought should be president. Then, the winner would be president, and the runner-up would be vice president.

NOT SO GREAT

This was very problematic. Imagine—the president and the vice president were usually from different parties and had different political opinions. And, they had just been rivals for the presidency. This was not a recipe for a good working relationship!

12TH TO THE RESCUE!

Now, each party nominates both the president and the vice president, meaning that the VP is no longer a disgruntled presidential wannabe! They work together as a team, and this is the system that we use to this very day.

I VOTE

I Voted

I VOTED FOR THE 1st TIME!

ELECTORAL COLLEGE

In America, the president and VP get elected by "electors," and NOT directly by the people. This can be really confusing— don't We the People elect the president and VP? Well, yes and no.

Every state gets a different number of electors, equal to the total number of their representatives and senators in Congress. These electors vote for the president. This gives more power to the small states. Otherwise, the people in the most populated states would have more control over who becomes president.

POPULAR V. ELECTORAL VOTE

With this system, a candidate can win the "popular vote" (by getting the higher number of votes from the people), but not be elected president if they don't win the "electoral vote" (by getting a lower number of votes from the state electors).

Confusing? For sure! Sometimes, election results do not represent what the people actually want because of the electoral college. Some feel that it is not an equitable system today, and that it should be abolished. What do you think?

Q. Which state has the highest number of electors?

A. Find the answer on page 97!

DID YOU KNOW?

There are **5 U.S. territories** that have the U.S. president as their head of state but do not have voting rights because they're not technically states. They are **Puerto Rico, Guam, American Samoa, U.S. Virgin Islands,** and **Northern Mariana Islands.** What do you think about that? *Should they have voting rights?*

Here's a way to visualize the **popular vote v. the electoral vote.** Imagine that Candidate A gets the full jar of candies on the left, and Candidate B gets the other two slightly filled jars. Who wins? Candidate B, because they got more jars (electoral votes)!

Candidate A lost, even though they got more candy (actual votes). In 2016, **Hillary Clinton** got more votes because more people in bigger states voted for her. However, she got fewer states overall to support her, so she lost the race. What do you think about this?

13TH AMENDMENT

Passed by Congress January 31, 1865. Ratified December 6, 1865.
A part of Article 4, section 2 was updated by the 13th Amendment.

★

ABOLITION OF SLAVERY AND INVOLUNTARY SERVITUDE

"NEITHER SLAVERY NOR INVOLUNTARY SERVITUDE, EXCEPT AS A PUNISHMENT FOR CRIME WHEREOF THE PARTY SHALL HAVE BEEN DULY CONVICTED, SHALL EXIST WITHIN THE UNITED STATES, OR ANY PLACE SUBJECT TO THEIR JURISDICTION."

The 13th Amendment made slavery illegal once and for all. This and the next two amendments are known as the "Civil War Amendments," made directly after and as a result of the Civil War. All three are supposed to give equal rights to formerly enslaved people. They intend to correct a major flaw in the Constitution previously, calling for the protection of the people under the federal government.

THE HYPOCRISY

The Constitution, up to this point, was supposed to protect ALL PEOPLE under the federal government. And yet, slavery was still legal! As you have learned, many white wealthy landowners—including some of the very men who wrote the Constitution—were slaveholders themselves. At the heart of the founding of this country was a huge disconnect, where the lofty ideals of freedom and human rights were in stark contrast to the violent and inhumane fact of slavery. The abolishment of slavery with the 13th Amendment was a step towards repairing this disconnect, which continues to affect our society in many ways today.

THE CIVIL RIGHTS ACT OF 1866

This act was able to be passed because of the 13th Amendment. It defined citizenship for all people born in the U.S. and affirmed that all citizens are equally protected under the law.

THE BLACK CODES, OR JIM CROW LAWS

There was a negative response to the 13th Amendment among powerful slaveholders in the southern states. They made laws that impeded Black people's freedom: for example, they could be arrested for a minor offense and punished with unpaid labor, essentially continuing the practice of slavery under another name.

EMANCIPATION PROCLAMATION

The 16th president, **Abraham Lincoln**, put forward the **"Emancipation Proclamation"** to end slavery in 1863. However, it wasn't legally binding and left a lot of open questions. Southern states—which benefited most from the transatlantic slave trade—ignored it. There was a need for a more binding solution.

This image represents a medallion designed for the British Anti-Slavery Campaign (Britain abolished slavery in 1833). The image went on to be part of the **abolitionist movement** in the U.S. as well.

AM I NOT A MAN AND A BROTHER?

THE TRANSATLANTIC SLAVE TRADE

The Translatlantic Slave Trade involved the transportation of about 12 million enslaved African people to North and South America. Of these, 600,000 were transported to America, 310,000 before 1776. Many wealthy white people at the time in America were slaveholders; this country was built with the labor of enslaved people. It's important to remember and learn about this history that still affects our society every day.

13th Amendment

HOW DID ABOLITION HAPPEN? IT STARTED WITH THE PEOPLE.

The abolitionist movement—the movement to end slavery—had both Black and white members, women and men. The abolitionists believed that "all men are created equal," no matter the color of their skin. They wrote petitions to the government and held meetings all over the country to fight for their cause.

END OF SLAVERY: A PROCESS

The abolitionist movement took place between 1830 and 1870, before and during the Civil War. Many people in the U.S., such as Lincoln, were anti-slavery but believed a gradual abolition process was needed. The abolitionists, however, always fought for immediate and complete abolition of slavery.

THE CIVIL WAR (1861–1865)

The northern and the southern states went to war over the question of slavery. The southern states had seceded from (left) the Union at that point and formed the Confederacy. The North was for ending slavery, and they won. Slavery was abolished and the Confederacy collapsed.

SOJOURNER TRUTH

Sojourner Truth was an abolitionist and women's rights activist, who traveled through many northern states and preached about equality. She felt that she was called upon to tell the truth (which is why she chose it as her last name).

Sojourner Truth was enslaved from birth, until an abolitionist family bought her freedom. She became known for her efforts and hard work for equal rights, and was invited to meet President Abraham Lincoln during the Civil War.

HARRIET TUBMAN

Harriet Tubman sought and gained freedom from slavery through a harrowing journey from the South where she lived, to the north where slavery was illegal. She went back to the South to help freedom seekers like herself, guiding them through the "Underground Railroad": a network of escape routes and secret hiding places set up by a group of abolitionists. She escorted over 300 people to freedom!

||||||||||||||
ABOLITION FAST FACTS
||||||||||||||

★ In 1827, leading up to the abolitionist movement, there were more antislavery organizations in the slave states than in the free states.

★ The American Anti-Slavery Society collected two million signatures in their 1838–1839 congressional petition campaign.

★ Angelina Grimké was the first woman in the U.S to ever address a legislative body—in the Boston State House in front of a huge crowd—on behalf of 20,000 Massachusetts women who signed antislavery petitions in 1838.

Q: What state was the first to abolish slavery?

A: Vermont, which abolished slavery in 1777.

14TH AMENDMENT

Passed by Congress June 13, 1866. Ratified July 9, 1868.

─────── ★ ───────

CITIZENSHIP, IMMUNITIES CLAUSE, DUE PROCESS, EQUAL PROTECTION

"... NOR SHALL ANY STATE DEPRIVE ANY PERSON OF LIFE, LIBERTY, OR PROPERTY, WITHOUT DUE PROCESS OF LAW; NOR DENY TO ANY PERSON WITHIN ITS JURISDICTION THE EQUAL PROTECTION OF THE LAWS."

The 14th Amendment protects the rights and freedoms of all citizens. With liberty and equality at its core, this superstar amendment is used in court more than any other!

HAPPY BIRTHDAY! YOU'RE A CITIZEN.

Birthright citizenship is established in this amendment. This means that ANYONE born on American soil—no matter their race, ethnicity, religion, tradition, ancestry, skin color, gender, you name it! Is an equal citizen of the United States.

EQUALITY

The 14th Amendment is all about equality. But does everyone have truly equal rights? Equity is a similar but different word that means giving everyone what they need to be successful. Different groups of people have different needs that must be met before we can have equality. Extra efforts should be made to ensure people know and can actually exercise the rights they have on paper.

PRIVACY

The 14th Amendment also talks about our right to privacy. This means that people have the right to make private choices about their lives. But what is privacy? Is who can we marry, for instance, a private choice? And who gets to make decisions about our health? Our society's view of privacy keeps changing! This Amendment is an example of the Constitution being understood in different ways as time goes by.

This amendment is the longest in the whole Constitution!

CHAMPION OF EQUAL RIGHTS: DR. MARTIN LUTHER KING JR.

Martin Luther King, Jr (aka MLK) was born in 1929 in Atlanta, Georgia, and grew up during segregation. He dedicated his life to the fight for equal rights regardless of race, color, or ethnicity. He travelled to India, and was greatly inspired by Ghandi, who preached about non-violent ways to create change in society. As a leader of the civil rights movement, MLK made speeches and sermons about peace and equality. His most famous speech is "I have a dream", about how everyone is created equal.

MLK was assassinated in 1958 while in Tennessee in support of a workers' strike. Today he is commemorated on MLK Day, around January 15 (his birthday). It is a day of service to give to our communities in his honor.

> **"** *I have a dream that one day this nation will rise up and live out the true meaning of its creed . . . that all men are created equal."*

DR. MARTIN LUTHER KING JR.

"I HAVE A DREAM" SPEECH IN FRONT OF OVER 200,000 PEOPLE IN WASHINGTON, D.C. IN 1963.

I have a DREAM

14th Amendment
★

The following groundbreaking Supreme Court cases used the 14th Amendment to make major shifts in American law.

BROWN V. BOARD OF EDUCATION
1954, KANSAS

In many states, schools were segregated, meaning Black kids went to separate schools from white kids with far fewer resources. Oliver Brown, along with a group of 12 other Black parents, went to court because their children were not permitted to attend the local school in Topeka, Kansas. Their case eventually made it all the way to the Supreme Court, who decided that "separate educational facilities are inherently unequal."

RESULT: Segregation outlawed!

LOVING V. VIRGINIA
1967, VIRGINIA

In 1959, Mildred Loving, an African American and Native American woman, and Richard Loving, a white man, were forced to leave Virginia because interracial marriage was illegal there. Their case made it all the way to the Supreme Court, which decided that "the freedom to marry, or not marry, a person of another race resides with the individual, and cannot be infringed by the State."

RESULT: Interracial marriage legal in all states!

OBERGEFELL V. HODGES
2015, OHIO

In 2015, Jim Obergefell and John Arthur married in Maryland because same-sex marriage was illegal in their home state of Ohio. They filed a lawsuit in Ohio, which led to a Supreme Court decision that legalized same-sex marriage in all 50 states.

RESULT: Same-sex marriage legal in all states!

CHAMPION OF EQUAL RIGHTS: RUTH BADER GINSBURG

Associate Justice of the U.S. Supreme Court, Ruth Bader Ginsburg is one of the biggest proponents of using the 14th Amendment in the legal fight against gender discrimination.

Born in New York City, RBG was a lawyer and a professor of law before becoming a judge. Her path to success was not easy though: throughout her career, she suffered gender discrimination, and made the battle against it one of her lifelong missions.

Fight for the things that you care about. But do it in a way that will lead others to join you."

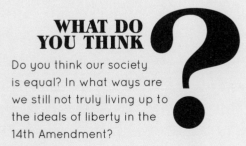
RUTH BADER GINSBURG

Q. Which was the first state to legalize same-sex marriage?

A. Massachusetts, in 2003!

WHAT DO YOU THINK ?

Do you think our society is equal? In what ways are we still not truly living up to the ideals of liberty in the 14th Amendment?

15TH AMENDMENT

Passed by Congress February 26, 1869. Ratified February 3, 1870.

★

VOTING RIGHTS

"THE RIGHT OF CITIZENS OF THE UNITED STATES TO VOTE SHALL NOT BE DENIED OR ABRIDGED BY THE UNITED STATES OR BY ANY STATE ON ACCOUNT OF RACE, COLOR, OR PREVIOUS CONDITION OF SERVITUDE..."

The 15th amendment was supposed to give Black men "enfranchisement", or the right to vote. However, technically it only prevented the state from denying them the right to vote, rather than actually giving them that right. This made it possible for states to get round the amendment, for example by charging people to vote through poll taxes, which very few Black people could afford.

ON PAPER

Many abolitionists had fought to give full citizenship rights—including political power—to Black Americans. They were finally successful, at least on paper, with the passing of the 15th Amendment.

IN REALITY

However, the REALITY is that the 15th Amendment was ignored and bypassed for almost 100 years! Black people were prevented from voting in most areas where they lived. Laws like imposing voting taxes and literacy tests were made in the South, which made it extremely difficult for Black people to vote.

FREDERICK DOUGLASS

Frederick Douglass was a leader in the abolitionist movement and a big supporter of the 15th Amendment. He was born in 1818 in Cordova, Maryland, into slavery; his mother was an enslaved woman and his father was white. As a boy, Frederick was taught to read by the wife of the slaveholder he worked for, even though that was illegal. When he was older, he sought his freedom in New York and became a writer, politician, and leader. He later went on to become an advisor to President Abraham Lincoln.

THE CIVIL RIGHTS MOVEMENT

Fast-forward to the 20th century. Black Americans were fed up with how they were being treated, so they formed the civil rights movement to fight for equality. Led by Dr. Martin Luther King Jr., Malcolm X, Rosa Parks, and many others, the movement gained momentum around 1955, following the Supreme Court case of *Brown v. Board of Education* (see page 74) and the Montgomery Bus Boycott, when many Black people in Alabama refused to use segregated buses in peaceful protest.

THE VOTING RIGHTS ACT

Even though the 15th amendment gave Black people the constitutional right to vote, we still needed to pass another law to make it a reality. In 1965, the civil rights movement led a huge march in Selma, Alabama to support Black voting rights. The marchers encountered a lot of violent opposition.

As a result, Congress passed the Voting Rights Act of 1965, signed by the 36th president, Lyndon B. Johnson, which outlawed racial discrimination in voting. Thanks to the civil rights movement, another step was taken towards equality.

Native Americans were denied the right to vote until 1924, and even then, it took over fifty years for states to recognize their right to vote with the support of the Voting Rights Act. Asian Americans didn't gain citizenship and the right to vote until 1952.

15th Amendment

★

Today, the fight for voting equality continues. There are still obstacles set in place by politicians that make it hard for some people to vote or make their votes count. This is called **voter suppression**.

GERRYMANDERING

Gerry who? This funny word for a not-funny practice is named after Elbridge Gerry, who was elected governor of Massachusetts in 1810. He signed a bill that supported creating a voting district in the shape of a salamander, which benefited his political party.

Gerry + salamander = gerrymander!

SO WHAT DOES IT MEAN?

Gerrymandering is a type of voter suppression, when a political group changes the borders of a voting district in order to change the outcome of an election. Sometimes the district has a really awkward shape, like Gerry's salamander-shaped district. It's usually due to systemic racism. Borders are drawn to keep all Black votes in one district, so that they don't influence the results of other districts. This limits their voting power, and it's not clear if it's legal or not. ***What do you think?***

FUN FACT!
LOW-EARTH ORBIT

NASA astronauts are able to vote from space! Thanks to "absentee ballots," they are able to send in their votes from the international space station. Their address is listed as "low-Earth orbit."

STACEY ABRAMS AND THE FIGHT AGAINST VOTER SUPPRESSION

In Georgia, politician and activist Stacey Abrams is leading the fight against voter suppression.

In some states, if someone's ID card has recently expired or has a misspelling, they can be turned away from the polls. Certain states also restrict people from voting if they owe a fine for having committed a crime. What do you think about this?

Sometimes rules like these are examples of blatant voter suppression. It's important to keep a close eye on rules that restrict voting, because voting is one of the greatest tools we have to make our voices heard and opinions count.

Gerry's original map. Cute, but not cute!

DID YOU KNOW?

Federal elections occur every two years, on the first Tuesday after the first Monday in November. In an election year, all members of the House and a third of the Senate are up for re-election. The presidential vote occurs every four years.

Q. Does everyone vote on election day?

A. No. People who cast an "absentee ballot" because they are living abroad (like U.S. service members) can sometimes vote before the official election day.

WHAT DO YOU THINK ?

Voting is not mandatory (required by law) in the U.S. Only about 60% of eligible voters (18+) turn out to vote! Do you think they should make a law that everyone must vote? Why or why not?

16TH AMENDMENT

Passed by Congress July 2, 1909. Ratified February 3, 1913.
Article 1, section 9 of the Constitution was modified by the 16th Amendment.

★

FEDERAL INCOME TAX

"THE CONGRESS SHALL HAVE POWER TO LAY AND COLLECT TAXES ON INCOMES, FROM WHATEVER SOURCE DERIVED, WITHOUT APPORTIONMENT AMONG THE SEVERAL STATES, AND WITHOUT REGARD TO ANY CENSUS OR ENUMERATION."

The 16th Amendment says everyone has to pay a certain amount of their income to the government. It's called income tax and it completely changed the federal government. It shaped America as we know it today and is the government's largest source of money!

Q: When is "Tax Day"? (Or, when do people need to submit tax returns to the federal government?)

A: Since 1955, Tax Day typically falls on April 15.

WHAT'S THE CONNECTION BETWEEN DEATH AND TAXES?

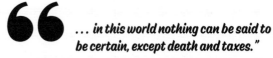

" . . . in this world nothing can be said to be certain, except death and taxes."

BENJAMIN FRANKLIN, 1789

Taxes have been around for a long time. Most governments take some money from their citizens in order to pay for big things that society needs. Franklin's famous joke about "death and taxes" above means that taxes are one of the only things in life that you can be sure you'll have to deal with, and they'll be around forever—just like death! A bit morbid, but it gets the point across.

A MORE POWERFUL NATION

Before this amendment, the federal government did not have a lot of money. It was weak and relied on small taxes on goods and imports. Originally, the framers did not want to pay lots of taxes to the central government because they didn't want it to get too powerful. However, over time, people realized that a weak and poor government couldn't do a lot. After the 16th Amendment, the U.S. grew into a world superpower. Having more money allowed the U.S. to do big things in the 20th century, like get involved in the world wars, advance scientific research, and go to the Moon.

In 1969, American astronaut **Neil Armstrong** became the first person to walk on the Moon!

WHAT DO TAXES PAY FOR?

Taxes pay for lots of different things, including healthcare, schools, national parks, transportation, the military and police, scientifc research, and having clean water in your home and the garbage collected from your street.

TOO MUCH OR TOO LITTLE?

Taxes are complicated. We have a **progressive tax system**, which means people pay according to their income. Many people don't like giving their money to the government. Some people feel like individuals are paying too much, while businesses pay too little. Some people think that rich people should pay more. Some people try to cheat and not pay at all! It can be very tricky and **controversial**.

DEBATE!
THE BIG TAX DEBATE

Consider the two viewpoints below. Think about them carefully or discuss them with a friend or family member. What do you think?

VIEWPOINT 1—MORE CAPITALIST:

Taxes should be low, and you should be able to keep most of your salary. The government should pay for things less, and businesses should handle most of the services (like medical care and transportation) instead. Rich people should not have to carry the burden of paying more taxes and supporting others.

VIEWPOINT 2—MORE SOCIALIST:

Taxes should be higher so that the government can offer lots of services to the people, like healthcare and education. Rich people should pay more taxes to help everyone else. This will build a more equal society between the rich and the poor.

17TH AMENDMENT

Passed by Congress May 13, 1912. Ratified April 8, 1913.
Article 1, section 3 of the Constitution was modified by the 17th Amendment.

★

POPULAR ELECTION OF SENATORS

"THE SENATE OF THE UNITED STATES SHALL BE COMPOSED OF TWO SENATORS FROM EACH STATE, ELECTED BY THE PEOPLE THEREOF, FOR SIX YEARS..."

BIG NEWS

Ever since the 17th Amendment, senators have been elected directly by the voters. But it wasn't always that way! Before this amendment, senators were chosen by state legislators (the group of people who make the laws in each state).

The 17th Amendment meant that senators would now be elected rather than selected, and represent the people directly, not the states. This gives more power to the voters.

WHY WAS THIS AMENDMENT CREATED?

1. To **avoid corruption** in the selection of senators, some of whom were chosen to further the interests of businesses and corporations.

2. To **combat inefficiency**: state legislators had disagreements over who should be chosen. This left Senate seats empty for long periods of time.

SENATOR FAST FACTS

Women:
To date, only **56 women** have served in the Senate, out of a total of roughly 1,982 people in all of American history!

Black folks:
To date, a total of only **10 Black men and women** have been senators.

Native Americans:
There have only ever been **6 Native American** senators.

LGBTQIA+:
For the first time, there are now **2 senators who openly identify as LGBTQIA+**.

SENATORS OF THE PEOPLE

CORY BOOKER

NEW JERSEY SENATOR

Senator Cory Booker grew up playing football. Before his time in the Senate, he was the mayor of Newark, New Jersey. In 2013, he became the first Black senator to represent New Jersey. Among other issues, Booker supports causes like women's rights and income equality.

Q: How many terms can a senator serve?

A. Each term is six years, and senators can serve for an unlimited number of terms!

Q: How many senators have become presidents?

A. 16 senators have become presidents. Three of them went directly from the senate to the White House—including Barack Obama, the 44th president.

TAMMY DUCKWORTH

ILLINOIS SENATOR

Senator Tammy Duckworth, in office since 2017, is an army war veteran. She is the first woman senator with a disability—she had both her legs amputated following a helicopter crash during her military service, for which she received the Purple Heart—the highest military award. Duckworth is also the first senator born in Thailand and the first senator to give birth during her time in office! As senator, Duckworth advocates for family and veteran rights, among other issues.

18TH AMENDMENT

Passed by Congress December 18, 1917. Ratified January 16, 1919. Took effect January 16, 1920.
Repealed by the 21st Amendment (see page 92).

★

PROHIBITION

*"... SALE, OR TRANSPORTATION OF INTOXICATING LIQUORS ...
THE IMPORTATION ... OR THE EXPORTATION ... FOR BEVERAGE
PURPOSES IS HEREBY PROHIBITED."*

Prohibition means something is forbidden by law. Per the
18th Amendment, no one was allowed to manufacture, sell, or
transport alcoholic beverages, including wine, whiskey, vodka,
liquors, and beer. However, alcoholic drinks used for religious or
medical reasons were allowed.

Prohibition was **repealed** 13 years later by the 21st Amendment.
This was the first and only time in American history that an
amendment to the Constitution was completely repealed.

IN COMPLIANCE
WITH THE
18th AMENDMENT
NO
INTOXICATING
LIQUOR
HERE!

PROHIBITION—WHY?

Many people thought that drinking alcohol could lead to bad things, and that it was morally wrong.

They thought that forbidding alcohol would:

* prevent problems caused by alcohol abuse, such as crime

* make people healthier

* prevent wild drunk behavior.

THE RISE OF THE "SPEAKEASY"

Prohibition forced saloons and bars to close their doors, but this didn't stop people from drinking alcohol. Lots of **illegal bars** opened secretly in basements of other shops, and in hidden rooms that were hard to find. Many would only let you enter if you had the right password, to make sure you weren't the police. These bars were called "speakeasies." The name comes from the need to speak quietly inside, so that the bar would stay a secret.

UNWANTED SIDE EFFECTS

In reality, it was hard to enforce Prohibition. People did not want to stop drinking alcohol, so they bought it illegally through a system known as the "black market." The result of Prohibition was the opposite of what people had in mind! Instead of a better-behaved society, a lot of people **broke the law** to make, sell, and drink alcohol.

PROHIBITION OF OTHER SUBSTANCES

Prohibition is long gone, but there are other substances that are forbidden, especially dangerous drugs. One substance that is highly contested is **marijuana**, which is illegal in many states. Many people want to legalize it nationwide.

Q: Which beer was allowed during Prohibition?

A. Root beer!

19TH AMENDMENT

Passed by Congress June 4, 1919. Ratified August 18, 1920.

★

VOTES FOR WOMEN

"THE RIGHT OF CITIZENS OF THE UNITED STATES TO VOTE SHALL NOT BE DENIED OR ABRIDGED BY THE UNITED STATES OR BY ANY STATE ON ACCOUNT OF SEX."

According to this amendment, no one can be denied the right to vote because of their gender. The 19th Amendment was presented 41 years in a row before it was passed. It's hard to believe that for so long women were not allowed to vote!

THE SUFFRAGETTES

The 19th Amendment was passed because of these women, who spent years fighting and protesting peacefully to gain **suffrage** (the right to vote). **Alice Paul and the Silent Sentinels** protested every day for two and a half years outside the White House. They were arrested and jailed, and then starved themselves in prison! Only then did Woodrow Wilson, the 28th president, take action to support the passing of the 19th Amendment.

THE SILENT SENTINELS created the ratification flag in the official colors of the Suffragettes—purple, white and gold (representing loyalty, purity and hope, among other reasons). They sewed on **36 stars**, one for each state that ratified the 19th amendment.

Q: How many women went to vote after the 19th Amendment?

A. More than eight million white women voted in the 1920 elections for the first time.

NOT EQUAL YET

The 19th Amendment was ratified in 1920, but not all women were able to vote. In some southern states, Black women couldn't vote up until the 1960s (see more about the Voting Rights Act of 1965 on page 77). In addition, Native American women and Asian women were only granted citizenship much later, which means they too could not vote in 1920.

THANKS, FEBB!

Dear Son,

With lots of love, Mama

Harry Burn was a conservative young politician from Tennessee who had previously voted against suffrage. In 1920, His mother, **Febb Burn**, wrote him a letter:

"Hurrah, and vote for suffrage! Don't forget to be a good boy and help Mrs. Catt*."

Burn surprised everyone by changing his stance. His vote tipped the scales in favor of the 19th Amendment! With his vote, it got the necessary majority of 36 states to pass.

* Referring to suffragist leader Carrie Chapman Catt

Q: When is National Women's History Week?

A. Every March, around International Women's day on March 8. The week was declared in 1980.

19th Amendment

INEQUALITY WITHIN THE WOMEN'S MOVEMENT

Even though women have gained a lot of rights and power over the years, progress is different for Women of Color and Native women. The women's movement has often put white **cisgender** women first and left Black and brown women, as well as LGBTQAI+ behind. White women as a group also still enjoy more advantages, for example, they get higher salaries (see more on page 11).

It is important to remember that Women of Color have been on the front lines of equal rights and women's movements, even if they were often overlooked. For example, before the *#MeToo* movement gained fame by white women, it was actually founded by social activist **Tarana Burke**, a Black woman, with the mission of helping young Women of Color who are survivors of sexual abuse.

INTERSECTIONALITY

Today there is a growing awareness and practice of "intersectional feminism." This means we put people who are affected by multiple levels of discrimination first, not last. It's about making room for EVERYONE.

The term **intersectionality** was coined by **Dr. Kimberlé Crenshaw** in 1989, and it is a way of looking at how our different identities affect oppression. Imagine the intersection of four streets—Race Street, Gender Boulevard, Sexual Orientation Way, and Location Avenue. A person standing in the middle is impacted by the oncoming traffic from all sides! In the same way, a person can experience discrimination for multiple parts of their identity.

Q: When were women first able to get a credit card on their own?

A. Only in 1974, with the "Equal Credit Opportunity Act."

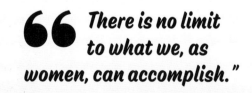

66 *There is no limit to what we, as women, can accomplish."*

MICHELLE OBAMA

WHAT DO YOU THINK ?

The fight for gender equality is not over yet. What do you think can be done?

100 YEARS OF SUFFRAGE FAST FACTS

The year 2020 marks the 100th anniversary of the 19th Amendment. There have been many improvements in women's rights over the last hundred years, but progress is mixed. Here are some examples:

★ Even though women earn more than **57%** of college degrees, they still only make up about **30%** of professors.

★ In 2018, for the first time, Native American and Muslim women were elected to Congress. However, women only make up **24%** of Congress. And there still hasn't been a woman president yet.

★ In business, there are still very few women CEOs of big companies.

★ Many women still make less money than men in the same jobs; this gap is even bigger for Women of Color than for white women (see more on page 11).

20TH AMENDMENT

Passed by Congress March 2, 1932. Ratified January 23, 1933.

★

COMMENCEMENT OF PRESIDENTIAL TERM AND SUCCESSION

"THE TERMS OF THE PRESIDENT AND THE VICE PRESIDENT SHALL END AT NOON ON THE 20TH DAY OF JANUARY, AND THE TERMS OF SENATORS AND REPRESENTATIVES AT NOON ON THE 3D DAY OF JANUARY … AND THE TERMS OF THEIR SUCCESSORS SHALL THEN BEGIN."

This amendment answered the question: When does the old president leave and when does the new one begin? The new timetable helped make the transition between the old and new government quicker and smoother.

CALENDAR CHAOS

Before this amendment, government timings were kind of odd. Elections took place in November, but the new president's term didn't start until March. The old president was a **"lame duck"** for five months, and the new president couldn't do much, either—it was a big waste of time!

The old timetable made sense back then, when it took forever for news (and people!) to travel anywhere. But in the 20th century, with trains, telegraphs, and telephones, things moved much faster and the old schedule made no sense anymore. **Things needed to speed up!**

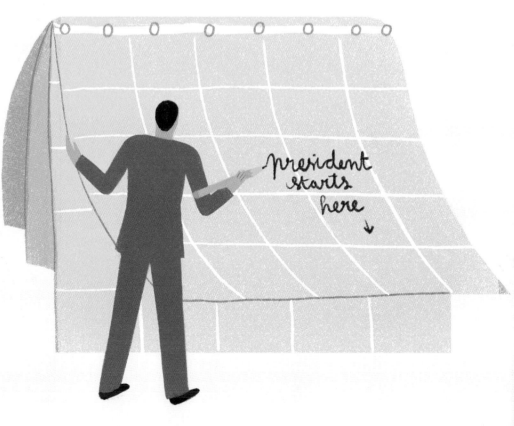

president starts here ↓

FUN FACT!
"LAME DUCK"

"Lame" is an old-fashioned term for when someone is unable to walk or move in a typical way because of an injury or illness. Imagine a duck who can't swim or fly. A president who is leaving office is called a "lame duck," because like the duck, they don't have full use of their previous power. They have less influence with the government because they have one foot out the door, and a new president has already been elected. On the other hand, some "lame duck" presidents have used this period to pass controversial laws because they knew they had nothing to lose!

THE WORST WINTER

After Franklin Delano Roosevelt was elected in winter 1932, he couldn't do anything to help with the **Great Depression**, because his term hadn't officially begun. The outgoing president, Herbert Hoover, was a "lame duck" and couldn't do much either. The country was in crisis, in one of the worst winters of the Great Depression, and it needed a leader to act! The 20th Amendment was passed in response, in order to shorten the "lame duck" period for future presidents by two months. It moved Inauguration Day, the day when the new president takes oath and starts their job, from **March to January.**

INAUGURATION

Usually, presidents are inaugurated in a big public ceremony in Washington, D.C., where they say an oath with their hand on the Bible. Some inaugurations were different, however. For example:

- **John Quincy Adams**, the 6th president, said the oath on a law book that contained the Constitution, instead of the Bible.

- **Lyndon B. Johnson**, the 36th president, was inaugurated on an airplane, immediately following the assassination of JFK.

Q: When in November do elections take place?

A. Turn to page 78 to find out!

IT'S ABOUT TIME

For years, Congress had tried to fix this problem with no luck. Between 1876 and 1924, over 70 different constitutional amendments were proposed in Congress to change the date for the government terms!

21ST AMENDMENT

Passed by Congress February 20, 1933. Ratified December 5, 1933.

★

REPEAL OF 18TH AMENDMENT

"THE EIGHTEENTH ARTICLE OF AMENDMENT TO THE CONSTITUTION OF THE UNITED STATES IS HEREBY REPEALED."

The American people are allowed to change their minds. Prohibition, which was implemented by the 18th Amendment (see page 84), was repealed 14 years later by the 21st Amendment. Amendments can't just be removed from the Constitution; a new amendment needs to cancel out the old one. This amendment is the ONLY one in the whole Constitution to do this.

New!
21st Amendment

18th Amendment

WHITE HOUSE SECRETS

Even during Prohibition, the White House did not stop Congress members from secretly ordering alcoholic beverages. The **bootlegger** who sold them the alcohol illegally was called the "Man in the Green Hat."

WHY WAS PROHIBITION REPEALED?

> 66 *"After fourteen years with nothing to drink the American people got thirsty."*

AN OLD JOKE ABOUT THE 21ST AMEMDMENT

When the 18th Amendment was passed back in 1919, many opponents of Prohibition predicted that it would **backfire**, and they were right! Criminals profited from selling alcoholic beverages on the black market and used their gains to corrupt government and law officials. Many people who once supported Prohibition changed their minds. It was hard to enforce, and alcohol became more of a problem than before. People realized it had been a **terrible mistake**.

BIG RETURNS ON THE 21ST AMENDMENT

In the first year post-Prohibition, the government collected more than **$258 million in alcohol taxes** alone! They couldn't do this during Prohibition, which meant a big loss to their income from taxes. This new money accounted for nearly 9% of the government's tax revenue, and it helped improve the economy during the Great Depression.

FDR ORDERS NEAR BEER

To show his support for ending Prohibition, FDR ordered two cases of "near beer" to the White House! This contained only 3.2% alcohol. Real beer usually has about 5% on average.

> 66 *"I trust in the good sense of the American people that they will not bring upon themselves the curse of excessive use of intoxicating liquors, to the detriment of health, morals and social integrity."*

FDR DECLARING THE END OF PROHIBITION

HOW DID PEOPLE CELEBRATE THE END OF PROHIBITION?

Some worried that people would go wild with excitement and drink too much post-Prohibition. However, according to the *New York Times*, "New York Celebrates with **Quiet Restraint** . . . Greenwich Village was almost somber in early evening; the sparkle had gone out of speakeasies turned legal."

UP TO THE STATES

The 21st Amendment gave the individual states the power to control their alcohol policies with the 18th Amendment. Federal government now has little control over alcohol production and consumption, and **policies vary widely across states**. For example, Mississippi kept laws prohibiting alcohol, and only ended Prohibition in 1966!

Q. What is the legal drinking age in the United States?

A. You have to be 21 to purchase alcohol or to drink alcoholic beverages in public.

22ND AMENDMENT

Passed by Congress March 24, 1947. Ratified February 27, 1951.

★

TWO-TERM LIMITATION ON PRESIDENT

According to this amendment, every president is allowed to serve for only two terms (one presidency term lasts for four years). In other words, the presidency is not forever. This is a way of limiting the president's power.

"NO PERSON SHALL BE ELECTED TO THE OFFICE OF THE PRESIDENT MORE THAN TWICE..."

WHY ONLY TWO?

George Washington, the 1st president, surprised everyone by stepping down after two terms. He wanted to show that he was different from a lifelong king or queen. For 150 years, Washington's behavior became the norm until the 32nd president, Franklin Delano Roosevelt, aka FDR.

FDR'S SUPER LOOOOONG PRESIDENCY

FDR was president for **12 years** (he would have served longer, but he died 11 weeks into his fourth term). He was the only president EVER to serve for more than two terms: he was elected four times!

So how come FDR had such a looooong presidency? One reason was that a big world war broke out during his second term. The American people wanted stability and they knew and trusted FDR to lead them during the hard times. They also did not want the turmoil of a new and unknown president in the middle of a war.

WHAT'S WRONG WITH MORE THAN TWO TERMS?

When FDR ran for the third time, some people started getting worried. They thought that he was gaining **too much power,** and that a long presidency was a threat to democracy. Time to give others a chance! The 22nd Amendment was proposed after FDR was elected for the fourth time, to make sure this wouldn't happen again. Since then, no president can serve for more than eight years.

Q. How many presidents served for two terms?

A. Only 13 presidents (out of 44) served for two terms. The rest (apart from FDR) served for only one term.

FDR ★ 32nd PRESIDENT ★ 1933–1945

ARE TIME LIMITS GOOD?

Not everyone loves this amendment. Several presidents have wished they could run for a third term! But more than that, scholars sometimes criticize this amendment for limiting the best people for presidency from doing their jobs, and for creating instability in the government.

What do you think?

Q: Which president had the shortest term?

A. William Henry Harrison, the 9th president. He died of an illness only 31 days into his presidency.

23RD AMENDMENT

Passed by Congress June 16, 1960.　　Ratified March 29, 1961.

★

DISTRICT OF COLUMBIA PRESIDENTIAL VOTE

"THE DISTRICT CONSTITUTING THE SEAT OF GOVERNMENT OF THE UNITED STATES SHALL APPOINT... A NUMBER OF ELECTORS OF PRESIDENT AND VICE PRESIDENT..."

Before this amendment, people living in Washington, D.C. couldn't vote for the president, because D.C. isn't technically a state! The 23rd Amendment changed that and made it possible for people of D.C. to vote for three "presidential electors," who vote on their behalf.

DID YOU KNOW?

The District of Columbia (D.C) is the capital of the United States. Back in 1790, Congress established it as the home of the U.S. government. They didn't want it to be in any state, so that it would belong to everyone.

So what is it? D.C is a **territory**—even though more people live there than in Wyoming and Vermont!

D.C. does not have any members of Congress—neither House nor Senate. It just has a delegate, but with no vote in Congress! Some people really want D.C. to become the 51st state so that it gets all the benefits that states do.

23RD AMENDMENT: WHY THEN?

The 23rd Amendment was passed during the height of the civil rights movement. Civil rights, such as the right to vote, were on everyone's minds. The people of D.C. demanded their right to vote!

ELECTORAL COLLEGE IN NUMBERS

The Electoral College is the group of people that represent the states in the election for president (see more on page 66). The EC has a total of **538** members. For a candidate to win, they need at least **270** electoral votes. Every state has a different number of electors, depending on its number of representatives in Congress. For example, New York has a total of **29**, and California has **55**—the highest number of electors! As we've seen, D.C. gets **3**.

FUN FACTS!
WASHINGTON D.C.

★ It's a very international place with more than 175 embassies.

★ It's one of the rainiest places in the U.S.

★ The phone number for the White House used to be "1."

★ The Library of Congress is the largest library in the world!

Q: Who was the first president to live in the White House in Washington, D.C.?

A. John Adams, the 2nd president. George Washington died a year before the White House was completed.

24TH AMENDMENT

Passed by Congress August 27, 1962. Ratified January 23, 1964.

★

ABOLITION OF POLL TAX REQUIREMENT IN FEDERAL ELECTIONS

"THE RIGHT OF CITIZENS OF THE UNITED STATES TO VOTE ... SHALL NOT BE DENIED ... BY REASON OF FAILURE TO PAY ANY POLL TAX OR OTHER TAX."

The poll tax was a sum of money that everyone needed to pay, no matter their income, in order to vote—this had been the case since the 1870s. The 24th Amendment overturned this rule. This ensures that everyone has a say, no matter how much money they have.

A TINY BIT OF HISTORY...

At first, only homeowners were allowed to vote. Later, it was expanded to anyone who could pay the "poll tax" (so, pretty much only rich people.) Eventually, most states got rid of these requirements and voting became available to all free white men (notice anyone missing?).

RACISM AND VOTING

Enter the 15th Amendment (see page 76), which allowed Black men to vote too. Some people didn't like this, so they set up obstacles like reading and writing tests to make it hard for Black people to vote. Sadly, they were successful. These barriers discouraged Black voters, many of whom were poor and uneducated due to the lasting impact of enslavement.

FIGHTING TO ABOLISH POLL TAXES

There were many efforts to abolish poll taxes, but none of them were successful. Finally, President Kennedy was able to pass the 24th Amendment in 1962, but only for federal elections.

It wasn't until 30 years later that the Supreme Court ruled that poll taxes were prohibited at the state and local levels too.

VOTE HERE FREE!

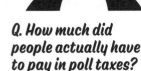

Q. How much did people actually have to pay in poll taxes?

A. Not very much—between $1 and $2 a year, but for some people this sum was discouraging.

THERE CAN BE NO ONE TOO POOR TO VOTE

PRESIDENT LYNDON JOHNSON

AT THE CEREMONY FOR THE 24TH AMENDMENT

25TH AMENDMENT

Passed by Congress July 6, 1965. Ratified February 10, 1967.
Article 2, section 1 of the Constitution was affected by the 25th Amendment.

★

PRESIDENTIAL VACANCY, DISABILITY, AND INABILITY

"IN CASE OF THE REMOVAL OF THE PRESIDENT FROM OFFICE OR OF HIS DEATH OR RESIGNATION, THE VICE PRESIDENT SHALL BECOME PRESIDENT."

What happens if the president dies? Or is too sick to do their job, or resigns? The vice president takes over! The 25th Amendment was added to clarify how this works.

A TRAGEDY LEADS TO AN AMENDMENT

This amendment was created when President John Fitzgerald Kennedy (JFK) was assassinated in 1963. Congress wanted to make an amendment that would explain in detail what to do if the president dies or can't do their job. In this case the vice president, Lyndon B. Johnson, took over.

THE 25TH AMENDMENT IN ACTION

Just a few years after this amendment passed, Vice President Spiro Agnew resigned. In the past, if a VP died or resigned, no one would fill their spot, but this time Richard Nixon, who was the president at the time, chose Gerald Ford to be his new VP. The story doesn't end there: that same year, President Nixon himself resigned, and Ford took over as president. This made him the only president in U.S. history who wasn't elected into office.

Q: In the history of the United States, how many times did the vice president become president as a result of the president's death?

A: A total of eight times.

66 *Ask not what your country can do for you, but what you can do for your country."*

PRESIDENT JOHN F. KENNEDY

John Fitzgerald Kennedy was born in 1917 in Brookline, MA. He said the words in this quote as part of a famous speech he made at his inauguration in 1961, when he was sworn in as America's 35th president. He served in office for only two years, because in 1963 he was assassinated (murdered in a surprise attack) by Lee Harvey Oswald,

in the middle of his term. In his short presidency, JFK proposed The Civil Rights Act of 1964, a super-important law against discrimination on the basis of race, gender, or religion. JFK was also a war hero, an animal lover, and a philanthropist: he donated all of his presidential salary to charity.

26TH AMENDMENT

Passed by Congress March 23, 1971. Ratified July 1, 1971.

★

THE RIGHT TO VOTE AT AGE 18

"THE RIGHT OF CITIZENS OF THE UNITED STATES, WHO ARE EIGHTEEN YEARS OF AGE OR OLDER, TO VOTE SHALL NOT BE DENIED OR ABRIDGED BY THE UNITED STATES OR BY ANY STATE ON ACCOUNT OF AGE."

This amendment brought down the voting age from 21 to 18.
This meant that young people would have more of a voice, as well as soldiers.

"YOU'RE OLD ENOUGH TO KILL, BUT NOT FOR VOTIN'"

During the **Vietnam War (1954–1975)**, many of the soldiers were younger than 21. They could carry weapons and kill, but they were not permitted to vote. Lots of people thought this was unfair. They protested, like in this line from the protest song "Eve of Destruction" from 1964. Congress came under pressure to allow soldiers this right, and they finally did.

❝ *The reason I believe that your generation, the 11 million new voters, will do so much for America at home is that you will infuse into this nation some idealism, some courage, some stamina, some high moral purpose, that this country always needs."*

PRESIDENT RICHARD NIXON
26th Amendment certification ceremony, 1971

SPEEDY 26TH

This Amendment was the quickest to be ratified ever! It was included in the Constitution just 3 months and 8 days after it was sent for ratification.

WHY THIS CHANGE?

These were some of the reasons Congress gave for why younger people should be given the right to vote:

★ Younger people are mature enough to vote.

★ They have all or most of an adult's responsibilities.

★ They should be given the chance "to influence our society in a peaceful and constructive manner."

What reasons would you add?

SO, DO THEY VOTE?

At first, many young people didn't vote. In recent elections, the numbers are increasing. Young people are having more and more influence on the results!

WHY ARE VOTING RIGHTS SO IMPORTANT?

Having the right to vote means you can choose your representatives and influence the government. The 26th Amendment protects voting rights and fights discrimination; in this case, ageism. It joins:

★ **The 15th Amendment** (see page 76), which prevents voting discrimination based on "race, color, or previous condition of servitude."

★ **The 19th amendment** (see page 86), which prevents discrimination on the basis of gender and gives women the right to vote.

★ **The 24th amendment** (see page 98), which eliminates poll taxes and prevents financial discrimination.

Q: Which was the first state to allow 18-year-olds to vote?

VOTE HERE →

VOTE

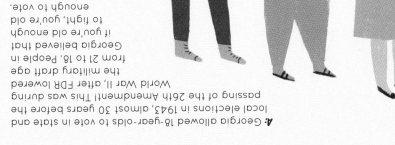

A: Georgia allowed 18-year-olds to vote in state and local elections in 1943, almost 30 years before the passing of the 26th Amendment! This was during World War II, after FDR lowered the military draft age from 21 to 18. People in Georgia believed that if you're old enough to fight, you're old enough to vote.

27TH AMENDMENT

Originally proposed September 25, 1789. Ratified May 7, 1992.

★

CONGRESSIONAL COMPENSATION

"NO LAW, VARYING THE COMPENSATION FOR THE SERVICES OF THE SENATORS AND REPRESENTATIVES, SHALL TAKE EFFECT, UNTIL AN ELECTION OF REPRESENTATIVES SHALL HAVE INTERVENED."

Finally, the last amendment (for now!). This final amendment is about limiting the power of Congress and state governments so that they are not allowed to raise their own salaries. Makes sense, right? But it took a very long time to pass it!

THE OLDEST AND THE NEWEST

Notice something weird about the dates? The 27th Amendment was proposed in **1789** but was not ratified until **1992**! That's more than 200 years later! So why didn't it pass in 1792? Because the framers disagreed about Congress' salaries. Some thought they should not be paid at all, while others thought that they should choose their own wage. Although the amendment was rejected in 1792, it had no time limit (which meant that it could be brought forward again!).

JUST THE RIGHT TIME

The ratification of the 27th Amendment happened at just the right moment in American history. In the 1980s, many people were critical of Congress. They thought they were getting paid way too much, and not doing their jobs well. So when the 27th Amendment was proposed, it wasn't too hard to convince many of the states to pass it.

THE POWER OF AN INDIVIDUAL: GREGORY GETS A C

Let's fast-forward to 1982. **Gregory Watson** was a student at the University of Texas. He wrote a college paper about the "Congressional Pay Amendment," (which was rejected back in 1792). He argued that since it had no time limit, it could still be ratified.

Guess what? Gregory got a C. His professor thought that there was no way this dead amendment could be revived. But Gregory was not having it. He decided to appeal his grade and prove his professor wrong. In 2017, he said in an interview with National Public Radio, "I thought right then and there, **"I'm going to get that thing ratified!"**

Gregory wrote letters to state legislators, who mostly ignored him. However, he didn't give up, and his hard work finally paid off when Senator William Cohen from Maine supported his idea. It became more and more popular until it was ratified in 1992 by the 38 states needed—more than 202 years after it was originally proposed! And there's another happy ending to the story: In 2017, the University of Texas FINALLY raised Gregory's grade from a **C to an A!**

Q. Presidents get salaries, too. It is required by Article 2 of the Constitution! But which three presidents have decided to forego their salary?

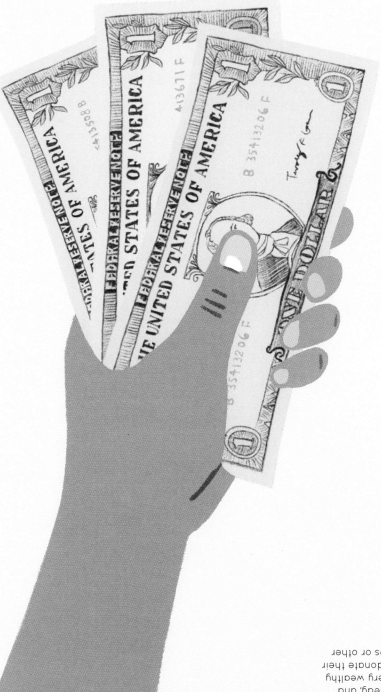

A. Herbert Hoover, John F. Kennedy, and Donald Trump all came from very wealthy backgrounds, and all chose to donate their presidential salaries to charities or other government agencies.

LOOKING FORWARD

You have now read about every single article and amendment of the Constitution. One of the most important things it teaches us is that every single person has power—not only queens, kings, presidents, and congresspeople. There are so many ways to take action for things you believe in. The power is in your hands! (See page 109 for further reading and resources.)

ACTIVISM

Anyone at any age can be an activist! Activism is when you take action to create political or social change. Here are some inspiring examples:

BOBBI JEAN THREE LEGS is part of the Lacota Sioux Native American tribe. She's fighting to protect her tribe's water supply and sacred grounds. She led a 2,000-mile run from North Dakota to Washington, D.C. to protest the threat to her tribe's lands. Her motto is "Mni Wiconi"—Water is Life.

JAZZ JENNINGS is an LGBTQIA+ rights activist. She has shared her story and experience as a transgender woman publicly, helping many people going through similar experiences as herself, and raises money for transgender children.

FUN!

Action is fun! Imagine the framers all those years ago—it was an exciting time because they were founding a brand-new country. Power is fun! Especially when you know you are creating a positive change in the world.

RESPONSIBILITY

We all have a responsibility to our communities and to each other. What are some small (or big!) steps you can take today to do something good for your community?

GETTING INTO POLITICS

There are many different ways to get involved with politics yourself. You can run for office at school. You can support a candidate by handing out flyers or making phone calls. You can organize or participate in a fundraiser for a cause you believe in. And when you're old enough, you can run for office!

Dear President,

"THE PERSONAL IS POLITICAL"

This was the rallying cry of the women's movement in the 1960s. And it's true! Politics affect everything in our lives. Like, how long a parent can stay home with a newborn baby, how much the minimum wage is when you get a job, whether the highways and subways are safe, and even having access to clean water and air.

What affects you personally that's also political?

PRIVILEGE

Some people have privilege (rights, freedoms, and benefits) that others do not, often just by being part of the majority. For example, able-bodied people enjoy the freedom of climbing stairs in buildings or transportation, while some people with disabilities don't.

Privilege can apply to race, color, religion, gender, sexual orientation, wealth, and more! And, a person can have privilege in one area, but not another. For example, a white woman has privilege in terms of race, but less in terms of gender because women are traditionally marginalized. Think back to "intersectionality" on page 88 to understand more about privilege. In what ways do you have privilege?

When taking political and social action, we need to remember that our own privilege can blind us to the needs of others. It's important to use our privilege to support others and take action that benefits everyone.

TIP: You can start to take action by getting behind a leader from a traditionally marginalized community!

IT'S OURS, SO WHAT SHOULD WE DO WITH IT?

The Constitution is interpreted differently every day. From the moment it was written, people have argued endlessly about what every word means, meant, or could mean. We have been pondering and wondering what the framers intended to say by this or that. Of course, we'll continue to interpret the Constitution in court cases. This is an amazing way it evolves with us—the same piece of text could mean something completely different for a case in the 1970s than it did for a case in the 1940s, and could mean something entirely different again in the 2020s.

WE ARE THE FUTURE

WHAT DO YOU THINK ?

But for now, outside of court, let's take a step back and look at the Constitution. Question it. Build on it. Replace it, maybe. What do you think we should do?

feminist

GLOSSARY

Abolition: The act of officially ending something, particularly slavery.

Activist: Someone who uses action, such as public protest, to support a cause or oppose an issue.

Advocate: (verb) To support or argue in favor of something. (noun) Someone who promotes the interest of a cause or group.

Amend: Make minor changes in a text in a formal way.

Assemble: Meet together, often in a particular place.

Bill: An idea for a law that is proposed.

Bill of Rights: A statement of formal rights, particularly the first ten amendments of the Constitution.

Censorship: Banning or removing parts of something such as a book or film.

Cisgender: Used to describe a person whose gender identity matches the sex they were assigned at birth.

Civil: To do with citizens. Civil law relates to private relations between members of a community.

Civil War: A war fought between groups who live in the same country.

Congress: The legislative branch of the U.S., made up of the Senate and the House of Representatives.

Delegate: (verb) Give or authorize. (noun) A person acting on behalf of another, such as a representative sent to a conference.

Demeaning: Taking away someone's dignity or making them feel inferior.

Democracy: A system of government where the people elect representatives to govern.

Dictatorship: A form of government where all the power is held by one person (a dictator) or a very small group.

Discrimination: To treat people differently or unfairly because of prejudice about something such as their race, sex, age, religion, or ability.

Emancipation: Freedom, particularly from slavery.

Executive: To do with the way laws are carried out and the branch of government that does this.

Federal: Used to describe a system where a number of states are ruled by a central government, but also have control over their own affairs.

Founding Fathers: The people who led the war of independence against Britain, united the 13 colonies, and laid the foundations of the new American government.

Framers: The people who wrote the original Constitution.

Great Depression: A time of economic crisis during the 1930s, which caused mass unemployment, hardship, and homelessness for many people.

Heteronormative: To do with the belief that humans are either male or female with associated gender roles.

House of Representatives: The lower house of Congress, with 435 members serving a two-year term.

Immunity: A special "shield" or protection. States in the U.S are protected from having a lawsuit brought against them by someone from another state or country.

Impeachment: When a public official, such as a president, is charged with criminal or corrupt behavior.

Inauguration: When a person with an important job, such as a president, is officially put into their position or "sworn into office."

Intersectionality: The complex way in which the different groups a person identifies with combine or overlap.

Judicial: To do with courts of law, and the branch of government that is made up of the Supreme Court and federal courts.

Law: An individual rule as part of a system.

Legislative: To do with making laws and the branch of government that does this.

LGBTQIA+: Stands for lesbian, gay, bisexual, trans, queer, intersex, asexual, plus all other sexualities and genders.

Petition: Make a request, often a formal written one.

Primary: An election in which people can vote for their party's candidate.

Ratify: Sign or agree to a treaty or contract in a formal way, making it official.

Repeal: Formally withdraw or cancel.

Segregation: The separation of people of different races or religions, whether by official government policy as in the U.S. before the Civil Rights Act of 1964, or in an unofficial systemic way.

Senate: The upper house of Congress, with two representatives per state who can serve unlimited six-year terms.

SEARCH & FIND

- How many American flags can you find?
- How many protestors holding signs can you find?
- How many elephants can you find?
- How many donkeys can you find?
- Find a kid wearing a shirt with the number 50.
- How many times are pickles mentioned in this book?
- How many yellow candies are in the book?
- How many presidents are depicted in this book?
- How many people getting married can you find?
- Add up all the money pictured in this book.
- How many babies can you find?
- Find the disembodied mustache.
- What time is it on the giant clock in this book?
- Find a sandy president.
- Find a queen.
- Find the red roses.
- How many pirates can you find?

FURTHER READING

BOOKS

This Book is Anti-Racist
by Tiffany Jewell

50 Trailblazers of the 50 States
by Howard Megdal

America's Bill of Rights
by Kathleen Krull

This is Our Constitution
by Khizr Khan

Start Now! You Can Make a Difference
by Chelsea Clinton

A Young People's History of the United States
by Howard Zinn

WEBSITES

Annenberg Classroom
annenbergclassroom.org
Videos and lessons to learn about the Constitution.

Oyez
oyez.org
Info about every Supreme Court case ever.

Constitution Center
Constitutioncenter.org
Lots of info about the Constitution!

Teaching Tolerance
tolerance.org
A great resource for teachers and students about activism and social engagement.

ACTION RESOURCES

Write to the president:
whitehouse.gov/contact

Commoncause.org
Enter your address to find all your representatives so you can email them or send them a postcard.

INDEX

The creators would like to thank: Mariana M. Cruz–Diversity & Inclusion Consultant, Lena Gilbert, Abby Wolf, Alessandra Biaggi, Ben, Sam, Pete and Teddy Sargent, Yitzhak, Nevae, Kayla and Romie Lewis.

Brimming with creative inspiration, how-to projects, and useful information to enrich your everyday life, Quarto Knows is a favourite destination for those pursuing their interests and passions. Visit our site and dig deeper with our books into your area of interest: Quarto Creates, Quarto Cooks, Quarto Homes, Quarto Lives, Quarto Drives, Quarto Explores, Quarto Gifts, or Quarto Kids.

First Published in 2020 by WIde Eyed Editions, an imprint of The Quarto Group.
100 Cummings Center, Suite 265D, Beverly, MA 01915, USA.
T (1)978 282 9590 F (1)978 283 2742 **www.QuartoKnows.com**

ISBN 978-0-7112-5404-6

The illustrations were created digitally
Set in Gotham Rounded, Grouch ITC, Vibur, Suti, Quicksand

Published by Georgia Amson-Bradshaw
Designed by Karissa Santos
Edited by Claire Grace and Rachel Minay
Production by Dawn Cameron

Manufactured in Guangdong, China TT042020

9 8 7 6 5 4 3 2 1